THE POLITICAL ECONOMY OF THE COMMON AGRICULTURAL POLICY

T0330611

What is the balance of the European Union's Common Agricultural Policy more than half a century after its birth? Does it illustrate the virtues of the European model of coordinated capitalism, as opposed to US-style liberal capitalism? Or is it an incoherent set of instruments that exerts diverse negative impacts and, like Frankenstein's monster, seems to have escaped the control of its designers?

The Political Economy of the Common Agricultural Policy does not criticize the CAP from the liberal standpoint that views most public interventions in the economy as bad for efficiency and welfare. The CAP has been costly to Europeans, both as consumers and as taxpayers, and has also generated a number of negative impacts upon third countries, but these costs and impacts have been more moderate than is suggested. This book proposes that the issue with the CAP is not a generic problem of coordinating capitalism but, instead, a more specific problem of low-quality coordination. The text argues that profound reform of the European Union's institutions and policies is required to counter the rapid rise of a more Eurosceptical state of mind but – in the case of agricultural policy – history casts serious doubts on the capacity of the European network of agriculture-related politicians to lead such a reform.

This key work is essential reading for researchers, graduate students, and master's level docents of the Common Agricultural Policy and – more broadly – European Union policy and reform.

Fernando Collantes is Associate Professor of Socioeconomic History at the University of Zaragoza, Spain. He has published widely on rural development and food systems from a historical perspective. He currently serves as a trustee of the Spanish Economic History Association.

THE POLITICAL ECONOMY OF THE COMMON AGRICULTURAL POLICY

Coordinated Capitalism or Bureaucratic Monster?

Fernando Collantes

Routledge
Taylor & Francis Group

LONDON AND NEW YORK

First published in English 2020
by Routledge
2 Park Square, Milton Park, Abingdon, Oxon OX14 4RN

and by Routledge
52 Vanderbilt Avenue, New York, NY 10017

Routledge is an imprint of the Taylor & Francis Group, an informa business

*¿Capitalismo coordinado o monstruo de Frankenstein? La política agraria común y el
modelo europeo, 1962–2020,* first edition –ISBN 978-84-8102-901-7-5–, was
originally published in Spanish by Cantabria University Press in 2019. This
translation is published by arrangement with Cantabria University Press.

British Library Cataloguing-in-Publication Data
A catalogue record for this book is available from the British Library

Library of Congress Cataloging-in-Publication Data
Names: Collantes Gutiérrez, Fernando, author.
Title: The political economy of the Common Agricultural Policy:
coordinated capitalism or bureaucratic monster? / Fernando Collantes.
Other titles: ¿Capitalismo coordinado o monstruo de Frankenstein? English
Description: Milton Park, Abingdon, Oxon; New York, NY: Routledge,
2020. | "¿Capitalismo coordinado o monstruo de Frankenstein? La política
agraria común y el modelo Europeo, 1962-2020, first edition,
ISBN 978-84-8102-901-7-5, was originally published in Spanish by
Cantabria University Press in 2019"—Title page verso. |
Includes bibliographical references and index.
Identifiers: LCCN 2019056952 (print) | LCCN 2019056953 (ebook) |
Subjects: LCSH: Common Agricultural Policy |
Capitalism–European Union countries. |
Agriculture and state–European Union countries.
Classification: LCC HD1918 .C6313 2020 (print) |
LCC HD1918 (ebook) | DDC 338.1/84–dc23
LC record available at https://lccn.loc.gov/2019056952
LC ebook record available at https://lccn.loc.gov/2019056953

ISBN: 978-0-367-85821-6 (hbk)
ISBN: 978-0-367-85820-9 (pbk)
ISBN: 978-1-003-01524-6 (ebk)

Typeset in Bembo
by Newgen Publishing UK

CONTENTS

FIGURES

TABLES

SUMMARY

What is the balance of the European Union's Common Agricultural Policy (CAP) more than half a century after its birth? Does it illustrate the virtues of the European model of coordinated capitalism, as opposed to US-style liberal capitalism? Or, conversely, is it an incoherent set of instruments that exerts diverse negative impacts and seems to have escaped the control of its designers?

This book uses a historical political-economy approach to answer these questions. The first chapter presents the conceptual framework of analysis, based on the notion of "varieties of capitalism", and revises the state of the art on the CAP. The second chapter describes the main policy instruments of the CAP, highlighting the difference between the CAP as a market-intervention policy (1962–1992) and the CAP as a direct-payments policy (1992 to the present). The following two chapters tackle the questions posed at the beginning. The third chapter questions the image, commonly presented by liberal economists, of the CAP as a "monster". The CAP has been costly to Europeans, both as consumers and as taxpayers, and has also generated a number of negative impacts upon third countries, but said costs and impacts have been more moderate than is usually suggested. The fourth chapter questions the alternative image, so dear to the European Commission, of the CAP as an illustration of the virtues of European-style coordinated capitalism. The idea that the CAP has inserted political values such as social equality, environmental sustainability and territorial cohesion in the functioning of Europe's agrarian capitalism is found to be an even greater myth. The fifth and last chapter explores the political causes of this dismal balance sheet and identifies the sources of deformation in the CAP's policy process over time.

This book does not criticize the CAP from the liberal standpoint that views most public interventions in the economy as bad for efficiency and welfare. The story of the CAP does not show that Europe's model of coordinated capitalism is inherently flawed. In fact, it is unlikely that a liberal, more market-oriented alternative would yield better results in social, environmental or territorial terms. The problem with the CAP is not a generic problem of coordinating capitalism, but a more specific problem of low-quality coordination. Giving an answer to the rapidly expanding Eurosceptical state of mind requires more than just making naïve statements about the alleged (but unproved) virtues of the European project, rather, it requires a profound reform of the European Union's institutions and policies. In the case of agricultural policy, history casts serious doubts on the capacity of the European network of agriculture-related politicians to lead such a reform. Therefore, it would be better if the CAP were incorporated in a broader, better-targeted food policy, as well as in the environmental and territorial policies that other, EU-level networks have been managing for three decades now.

INTRODUCTION

What ever happened to the eagerness for the European Union? Barely a decade ago, excitement and optimism reigned. The former contenders in the Second World War had made it – they had put their economic interests in common and that had allowed them to move forward in the construction of common political institutions. The six founding-member states had succeeded at handling competently the incorporation of more than twenty other countries from all parts of Europe that were willing to be a part of such an exciting project. The public opinion showed a remarkable degree of satisfaction with the European Union and, in those occasions when they were consulted by their respective governments, electorates tended to position themselves as pro-European (Dedman 2010: 163).

Today, conversely, Euroscepticism is on the rise. The early years of the new millennium brought some signs of a new trend, as the electorates in a number of countries refused to accept EU proposals set to reinforce the political integration of the Union. Of particular significance was the fact that, within the historical hard core of the EU, voters in France and the Netherlands voted no to the treaty for a European constitution (Dedman 2010: 163–164). But it was mostly the economic crisis that started in 2008 that drove Euroscepticism higher than ever before. The EU has been badly affected by the internal tensions stemming from the political management of the crisis, as well as by the spread of broader criticisms on the grounds of its political networks' lack of effectiveness and legitimacy (Tooze 2018). With the triumph of "Leave" over "Remain" in the so-called Brexit referendum, Eurosceptics have achieved a major victory in the United Kingdom, while recent elections in countries such as France, the Netherlands and Italy (three of the founding member states) have provided them with new causes for celebration.

In ways that may differ slightly from country to country and from one end of the political spectrum to the other, Eurosceptics complain that the European Union is a constraint, rather than an opportunity. Some of them are nationalists who argue that their countries have come to be governed from Brussels and that leaving the EU is the way to give the power back to democratically elected, national leaders. Others are left-wingers who argue that the EU is just another word for neoliberalism, and that leaving it behind is a means to preserve the European tradition of socially responsible capitalism.

In between remains a wide space covering everything from the centre-left to the centre-right, and which watches with perplexity the breakdown of pro-EU consensus. Its strategy is basically to argue that Euroscepticisms are nothing but unfortunate populisms, and that we should just wait for the storm to pass. After all, Eurosceptics have triumphed in the United Kingdom but, in spite of all their growth in numbers, they have not even come close in France or the Netherlands. Nor were they able to prevail within the Syriza-led Greek government at the critical juncture of 2015. In the end, therefore, everything will be okay because we are right: you really need to be (and feel like) a "globalization loser" in order to pay attention to irresponsible populist agitators and fail to see that the EU incarnates humanity's most honourable values.

This response to Euroscepticism is basically unsatisfactory because it is defensive, and what the Eurosceptical questions require is active answers. We are talking about truly key questions. Is the EU really a triumph of democracy or, on the contrary, an institution with a serious problem of lack of legitimacy? Is it a bastion of Europe's tradition of social capitalism within a global neoliberal era or, conversely, an agent working against said tradition? Eurosceptics may not be right in their own answers to these key questions about democracy and capitalism. It may also be the case that, even if their answers are right, the practical implications Eurosceptics draw from them are faulty. But they are posing the right questions. The EU is in danger of sinking in an anti-populist complacency that overlooks the fact that, independently from who is posing these questions, they need convincing answers instead of simplistic slogans. The Eurosceptical opposition needs to be synthetized, incorporated, rather than simply dismissed.

This book analyses the socio-economic dimension of the problem through a case study of the Common Agricultural Policy (CAP). This is one of the oldest and most important policies of the EU. Historically it has been the main common policy and, still today, when farmers are but a tiny fraction of Europe's active population (less than 5 per cent), it remains EU's second most-expensive policy. Only the regional cohesion policy absorbs a larger share of the EU budget, and not even on the horizon is there any serious contender to the CAP's second place in the ranking. The core of the political discussion between member states may have shifted towards other areas, such as the aforementioned regional policy or (for those countries belonging to the euro area) the management of the common currency, but the making of each new reform of the CAP still manages to produce major political tensions in Brussels. In a way, as historian Tony Judt (2011: 23) argues, the CAP "can stand as a metaphor illustrating the whole enterprise of 'Europe'".

After this introduction, the first chapter of the book positions the debate on the CAP within a broader debate on "varieties of capitalism" and Europe's so-called economic and social model. The second chapter contextualizes the analysis by presenting a basic history of the measures that have formed the CAP over the years. The following two chapters examine the socio-economic impacts: the third chapter explores the costs and problems created by the CAP, while the fourth assesses its potential benefits and contributions. After that, the fifth and final chapter explains the political process that underpinned the making of the original CAP, as well as later reforms of it. The book's epilogue rearranges these pieces in a chronological narrative, an extension of which is a series of forward-looking recommendations.

The analysis is framed within a historical political-economy approach. This means basically two things. First, we rely on a conceptual framework that differs from that of orthodox economics. As the Cambridge school of social ontology argues, it is far from obvious that the premises of orthodox economics, in particular methodological individualism and mathematical formalization, are well suited to the nature of the social reality that it is supposed to study (Lawson 1997, 2005). In consequence, a more promising alternative may be to reinvigorate and develop the older tradition of a "political economy" in which the economic is more deeply embedded within the social and the ethical (Martins 2013). This alternative, however, is not oriented towards replacing orthodox economics within its own field as much as towards an interdisciplinary social science that is able to move the analysis to a more inclusive field in which sociology, geography and history play an important role (Stilwell 2019). The term "socio-economics" has also been used recently in order to refer to this approach (Hellmich 2017).

The historical political-economy approach of this book also means another thing: an adhesion to the notion of "historical social science" (Wallerstein 1977, 1991). History is interesting in itself, but it is also a method of analysis that gravitates around the evolution of social systems in the long run. This does not imply dismissing shorter-run historical movements, but it does lead to relativizing their importance in favour of a longer-run analysis, the outcome of which does not necessarily have to match the mental frameworks of historical protagonists. Several currents in social science, especially in economics and political science, are recently experiencing a historical turn that is in line with this view (Freeman and Loucã 2001; Hodgson 2001; Piketty 2014; Fioretos et al. 2016).

Out of this historical political-economy approach come the two main novelties of this book as an analysis of the CAP. First, the book tries to consider the socio-economic and the political sides of the analysis in a more integrated fashion than has been common so far. We have a sizeable literature on each of these two spheres, but few connections have been made between them. Some of the best economic studies, such as those by Michael Tracy (1989) and Giovanni Federico (2009), have little to say about the political underpinnings of the CAP, while the best political studies, such as those by Alan Milward (2000) and Ann-Christina Knudsen (2009), do not delve into the socio-economic consequences of the political decisions taken. This book is mostly focused on the socio-economic side, but it also aims at understanding the underlying political dynamics. In this sense, it is closer to the approach of Niek Koning (2017) and Philip McMichael (2013), who contribute, however, global analyses that do not extensively consider the particular case of Europe's CAP.

Secondly, the book aspires to providing a longer-run perspective than is usual in most available historical and social science studies, not to speak of journalistic coverage of the CAP. By favouring recurrent, long-run dynamics over shorter-run developments, this may lead to interpretations and explanations that differ from those that dominate the literature. Again, some of the best studies of the CAP are particularly strong in the short run. Historians like Knudsen and Federico, for instance, are very comfortable within CAP's initial phase but, even if they are not unfamiliar with the changes that took place afterwards, their analysis integrates said changes as a modest epilogue set to reinforce the original conclusions. Other important studies in economics and political science, such as those by Arlindo Cunha and Alan Swinbank (2011) and Marko Lovec (2016), focus mostly on the recent era of CAP reforms and, even if they know about CAP's earlier history, they use the latter basically as a context-providing prologue. This book has the aspiration of offering for the first time a synthesis that integrates in a balanced way CAP's different historical periods within a longer-run analysis. In this sense too, it is more in line with the broader approaches to agricultural policy used by Koning or McMichael, as well as by Adam Sheingate (2001).

In return for this, the book exacts a considerable price from its readers: it does not give them a complete, once-and-for-all history of the CAP. Here there is no thick description of the short-term developments that are also part of the CAP's history. Nor is there an exhaustive narrative about the many policy details that, at each moment in time, seemed important to policymakers, social agents and scholars, but that have failed to stand the test of time as key interpretive elements (or at least have failed to do so in relation to the issues posed by this book). My personal favourite is the "green exchange rates", the complex system that the European Economic Community (EEC) designed in order to (try to) harmonize agricultural support among countries in a world of floating exchange rates. It has been said that the chancellor of the Federal Republic of Germany once complained that the only one of his officials who understood the green money system was not able to explain it to him, while the official who was capable of explaining it did not really understand it (Eichengreen 2007: 184). Undoubtedly, a full history of the CAP should include this and many other policy mazes, such as the asymmetries in the application of the CAP among member states and commodity groups. The objective of this book is different: it aims to use history in order to construct a general argument about the CAP. The book is, therefore, closer to a history-based essay than to a history monograph proper.

Who, then, is the target readership of this book? In the first place, the book may be useful for graduate students and master's-level docents who need a text that is both synthetic and analytical in order to enter the complex world of the CAP. Textbooks tend to offer an excessively schematic treatment, while the specialized literature that defines the research frontier induces a justified sensation of vertigo among the non-initiated. This book could be an intermediate point between both worlds. Furthermore, and for the same reason, the book could be useful for those researchers who need to know more about the CAP for instrumental reasons. It is only a slight exaggeration to say that nearly any investigation of Europe's agriculture and rural society during the last half century needs some transversal familiarity with the CAP, since this policy has critically shaped the framework in which farmers and other social actors have made their decisions. Most researchers, though, also feel uncomfortable with the void that currently exists between the generalities of textbooks and the very fragmented debates of CAP specialists. This book could provide them with a reference point they may find more useful. Finally, by framing the debate on the CAP within a broader debate on Europe's model of coordinated capitalism, I have also sought to capture the attention of readers interested in the latter, as well as to move CAP specialists to consider the wider ramifications of their conversation.

Acknowledgements

I have written this book over a prolonged period of time, during which I had the chance to work with students from the master's programme in European Union studies of the University of Zaragoza, Spain. My relationship with them had a great influence on the book's orientation. The fact that over the years I had to teach the CAP under three different European commissioners of agriculture and three different versions of the policy convinced me of the need to provide students with an analysis of fundamentals rather than a description of details. Details, after all, are constantly changing. In some particular years, I had the sensation that there was a real danger to supplying a large amount of information that was set to become completely irrelevant as the semester was going by. The point was to offer students something that could be useful for them to understand not only the past and the present, but also a future that was not yet written but would surely be different.

In addition, I was lucky that most students had not been trained in economics. Some of them had, or at least were graduates in, business studies. But most were coming from degree programmes as diverse as law studies, journalism, labour relations, sociology, geography, history and international relations. For those of my colleagues who were willing to apply the theoretical instruments of mainstream economics to the analysis of the European Union, this was understandably a nuisance. I always, however, experienced it as the perfect excuse to use a more inclusive framework of analysis. Explaining the CAP to non-economists was a challenge, and one that I was not always able to meet in a fully successful way, but it brought me closer to writing this book. The same applies to the fact that a substantial portion of my students were coming from countries that did not belong to the EU's hard core – such as Italy, Greece, Bulgaria and Romania – or not belonging to the EU at all, such as China.

Among the colleagues, my first acknowledgment is for Ramón Barberán, the first coordinator of the masters programme on European Union studies and responsible for my starting to teach about the CAP. I also thank the flexibility shown by my other teaching mates at the course on the EU budget in which my CAP lectures were included: Luis Antonio Sáez, María Jesús Mancebón, Sara Barcenilla and Chema Gómez.

I am very grateful to the colleagues who, over the months prior to the culmination of the Spanish version of this book, helped me in diverse ways to complete it. Miguel Martín-Retortillo, Vicente Pinilla and an anonymous referee from the Spanish publisher (University of Cantabria) made very constructive comments on an early version of the text. Niek Koning and Adam Sheingate were kind enough to engage in correspondence about several ideas that came to me after reading their work. This does not mean, of course, that they can be held responsible for any of the arguments made in the book. The same can be said in relation to Victoriano Calcedo, with whom I had the chance to continue a conversation that started some twenty years ago when, as an undergraduate student, I attended his lectures on the CAP. Finally, Jesús María Valdaliso invited me to present my views in a seminar on the CAP at the University of the Basque Country, during which I received very useful feedback from an audience of historians and economists.

I would also like to thank Albert Herreria for his fantastic, meticulous work on my English. Thanks also to the Routledge editorial team, especially Andy Humphries, for supporting this project at an early stage and working so efficiently to move it forward, and Emma Morley, as well as the anonymous referees.

My last acknowledgment goes, of course, to my wife Elena and our children Diego, Ana and Álvaro. I am lucky to share my life with them and find that this life in common sets strict, and yet joyful, limits to my time available for working on a project such as this one. Who knows if this was probably better for the book itself, forcing it to become more synthetic and direct. But what I am sure of is that it was better for me – much better than I can now awkwardly try to express in a few inadequate words, and it is with all my heart that I thank them for it.

References

Cunha, A. and Swinbank, A. 2011. *An inside view of the CAP reform process: Explaining the MacSharry, Agenda 2000, and Fischler reforms*. Oxford: Oxford University Press.

Dedman, M. 2010. *The origins and development of the European Union 1945–2008*. Abingdon: Routledge.

Eichengreen, B. 2007. *The European economy since 1945: Coordinated capitalism and beyond*. Princeton: Princeton University Press.

Federico, G. 2009. "Was the CAP the worst agricultural policy of the 20th century?". In *Fertile ground for Europe? The history of European integration and the Common Agricultural Policy since 1945*, ed. K. K. Patel, 257–271. Baden-Baden: Nomos.

Fioretos, O., Falleti, T. G., and Sheingate, A. 2016. "Historical institutionalism in political science". In *The Oxford handbook of historical institutionalism*, eds. O. Fioretos, T. G. Falleti and A. Sheingate, 3–30. New York: Oxford University Press.

Freeman, C. and Louçã, F. 2001. *As time goes by: From the industrial revolutions to the information revolution*. Oxford: Oxford University Press.

Hellmich, S. N. 2017. "What is socioeconomics? An overview of theories, methods, and themes in the field". *Forum for Social Economics* 46 (1): 3–25.

Hodgson, G. M. 2001. *How economics forgot history: The problem of historical specificity in social science*. London: Routledge.

Judt, T. 2011. *A grand illusion? An essay on Europe*. New York: New York University Press.

Knudsen, A.-C. L. 2009. *Farmers on welfare: The making of Europe's Common Agricultural Policy*. Ithaca, NY: Cornell University Press.

Koning, N. 2017. *Food security, agricultural policies and economic growth: Long-term dynamics in the past, present and future*. London: Routledge.

Lawson, T. 1997. *Economics and reality*. London: Routledge.

Lawson, T. 2005. "The nature of heterodox economics". *Cambridge Journal of Economics* 30 (4): 483–505.

Lovec, M. 2016. *The European Union's Common Agricultural Policy reforms*. London: Palgrave Macmillan.

McMichael, P. 2013. *Food regimes and agrarian questions*. Winnipeg: Fernwood.

Martins, N. O. 2013. *The Cambridge revival of political economy*. London: Routledge.

Milward, A. S. 2000. *The European rescue of the nation-state*. London: Routledge.

Piketty, T. 2014. *Capital in the twenty-first century*. Cambridge: Harvard University Press.

Sheingate, A. D. 2001. *The rise of the agricultural welfare state: Institutions and interest group power in the United States, France, and Japan*. Princeton: Princeton University Press.

Stilwell, F. 2019. "From economics to political economy: Contradictions, challenge, and change". *American Journal of Economics and Sociology* 78 (1): 35–62.

Tooze, A. 2018. *Crashed: How a decade of financial crises changed the world*. New York: Penguin.

Tracy, M. 1989. *Government and agriculture in Western Europe, 1880–1988*. New York: New York University Press.

Wallerstein, I. 1977. "The tasks of historical social science: An editorial". *Review* 1 (1): 3–7.

Wallerstein, I. 1991. *Unthinking social science: The limits of nineteenth-century paradigms*. Cambridge: Polity Press and Blackwell.

1

THE "EUROPEAN MODEL OF AGRICULTURE" ON TRIAL

According to economist Louis Malassis (1997: 196), "the CAP provides a good example of the system of mixed, regulated economy that in different degrees triumphs everywhere in developed countries after the war". The CAP has always been such a complex policy that researchers have understandably been busy enough trying to analyse it on its own terms. However, the debate on the CAP belongs to a larger one: What is the optimal combination of market freedom, on the one hand, and public intervention, on the other? Is "coordinated capitalism" superior to "liberal capitalism"? Is the "European model" to be preferred to the "American model"? Is it good news that the developed economies have shifted from public intervention to deregulation in the last few decades? In no small measure, the participants in the CAP debate make their contributions from a standpoint defined by their positions in these broader controversies.

This chapter is organized as follows. After this introduction, the first section presents the debate on the European model and positions it within the theoretical discussion of "varieties of capitalism". The second section describes the highly positive assessment made by the European Commission (and much of public opinion) of the CAP and the "European model of agriculture" that is allegedly embedded in that assessment. The rest of the chapter considers the arguments presented by academic researchers. The third section reviews the most frequent criticisms raised by mainstream economists, whereas the fourth section surveys the views held by other scholarly communities. Finally, the fifth section concludes by offering a synthesis of the evolution of the CAP controversy over time.

Europe and "coordinated capitalism"

The debate on the so-called European model has been prominent since the turn of the millennium. For historian Tony Judt (2005: 7–8), an eclectic mix of Social

Democratic and Christian Democratic policies would have come to define "a distinctively 'European' way of regulating social intercourse" that would be in sharp contrast to the American way of life. Economist Barry Eichengreen (2007: 4), for his part, argues that European capitalism is a "coordinated capitalism", in contrast to the liberal capitalism of the United States. For Eichengreen, European capitalism has historically required "a set of norms and conventions [...] to coordinate the actions of the social partners and solve a set of problems that decentralized markets could not". Markets in Europe would function less freely than in America: Europe's policies of competition protection would be more moderate, while factor markets (for both labour and capital) would be more tightly regulated by the state and by a myriad of formal and informal arrangements between numerous stakeholders. Europe's coordinated capitalism would also feature more drastic redistributive policies than those of the United States. These distinct "norms and conventions", following Eichengreen's formulation, would operate on several different territorial scales, including here the supranational scale represented by the institutions of European integration.

The European Union vindicated this economic and social model as a central element of its identity in the Lisbon Treaty of 2007, which was meant to redefine the principles and functioning of the Union. In article 2.3 of the Treaty, the EU expressed its preference for a "social market economy". This notion, deeply rooted in the political culture of many member states, captures the essence of coordinated capitalism: the attempt at combining a market economy with public interventions and nonmarket arrangements designed to improve the former's capacity to attain socially desirable objectives. In the case of the Lisbon Treaty, these objectives would be primarily social justice, environmental protection and territorial cohesion.

This identification of coordinated capitalism (or the social market economy) as a distinctively European model is important because it has been taken for granted as a necessary premise in the debate about whether the model, and therefore the EU, works or not. For economists such as Alberto Alesina and Francesco Giavazzi (2006), the model does not really work and Europe, damaged by an overregulated economy, should embark on an ambitious structural reform in order to make its economy more flexible. If Europe does not transform its coordinated capitalism into something more similar to the US model of liberal capitalism, it will not be able to halt Europe's ongoing decline in economic and political terms on a global scale.

Other opinions have been less radical, but doubts have been raised by all sides about the degree to which the European model is compatible with the imperative of international competitiveness within a multipolar global economy. The European Commission itself commissioned an analysis of this to a group of economists led by André Sapir. The starting premise of the Sapir group was that, even though the European model had managed to retain a remarkable focus on social equality, its economic growth record had been disappointing. The final conclusion was that the EU needed deep reforms in governance and in the nature of its economic and social policies, which should be redefined in order to provide a more propitious environment for corporate investment and economic growth (Sapir et al. 2004).

Even the most nuanced analysts have cast doubt on the capacity of Europe's coordinated capitalism to survive unless it is substantially reformed. Eichengreen (2007), for instance, argues that the degree of fitness of Europe's coordinated capitalism depends on the context. During the decades after the Second World War, when Europe's economies were lagging behind the United States, coordinated capitalism would have favoured Europe's capacity to absorb American technology and converge rapidly in relation to the American level of GDP per capita. However, European institutions would have been much less growth-friendly at a later stage, from the 1970s onward, as the opportunities for that kind of "extensive" growth faded away and Europe needed to move towards "intensive" growth based on endogenous innovation. In this new context, institutional rigidities would be preventing Europe from achieving a growth performance comparable to that of the United States. Contrary to others, Eichengreen concludes that Europe has the right fundamentals to keep on growing, and that the European model may even have a chance to survive but, similar to others, he links that to the implementation of flexible reforms.

Not everyone agrees with this line of analysis, though. To begin with, is Europe's coordinated capitalism really exceptional in today's global economy? The notions of coordinated and liberal capitalism are usually taken from the influential work of political scientists Peter Hall and David Soskice (2001), who did not however apply them on a macroeconomic scale. In Hall and Soskice's analysis, the difference between both types of capitalism has more to do with a microeconomic vector composed of variables such as labour market institutions, the connection between finance and the rest of sectors, and the relationships of cooperation and competition between firms. But what happens when we position the contrast between different "varieties of capitalism" within a more macroeconomic perspective? The result is that, as has been argued by the French regulation school (Boyer 2005), there are more varieties of capitalism than just two. Even if we limit the analysis to Organisation for Economic Development and Cooperation (OECD) countries, there would be at least four types of capitalism: not only market-oriented, as in Anglo-Saxon countries, and state-coordinated, as in much of continental Europe, but also "meso-corporatist" capitalism in Japan and Southeast Asia and social-democratic capitalism in Scandinavia. Seen this way, the exceptional variety of capitalism, the one that is less similar to the other three, is Anglo-Saxon liberal capitalism, whose reliance on the free market contrasts to the way in which all three other varieties of capitalism rely on public and private nonmarket arrangements in order to shape the social adjustments derived from economic change. This regulationist perspective, however, has been ignored by the mainstream economists who have so far dominated the debate on Europe's coordinated capitalism and its future.

Other, unrelated, studies have also made contributions that in different ways call into question the very premise of the debate. Some, for instance, have raised doubts about the degree to which the United States really illustrates the alleged connection between liberal capitalism and technological innovation. After all, the Schumpeterian school of "national systems of innovation" had always argued that the causes of innovation have to do with business organization, social context and public policies rather than with market freedom per se (Freeman 1995). For economists such as Mariana Mazzucato (2013), public policies have been crucial for the United States to remain at the global forefront of innovation in the current age of information and communication revolutions. An important implication for the varieties of capitalism debate is that there is probably less opposition between coordinated and non-coordinated capitalism than a contrast between different ways of coordinating capitalism, each of them based on different values, objectives and procedures.

While Schumpeter's followers move us to a less-idealized view of the United States as the mecca of liberal capitalism and pro-market orthodoxy, a comparative analysis of the economic crisis that started in 2008 moves us to be equally cautious about the degree to which Europe really represents a variety of capitalism that is tightly controlled by public policy. As argued by historian Adam Tooze (2018), the crisis was in large measure a crisis derived from the integration of the ever more deregulated financial systems of the United States and Europe. Precisely because of this, it would have shown that, underneath their own discourse about an alleged social market economy, Europeans had in large measure the same kind of "turbo-charged financial capitalism" as the Americans. And, the argument goes on, if we compare the policy responses to the crisis on both sides of the Atlantic, we find that it was Europe, not the United States, that chose the more orthodox agenda.

None of this questions the convenience of debating about Europe's coordinated capitalism, but it does question that the debate should be essentially about whether a European anomaly called coordinated capitalism, standing in frontal contrast to US-style, orthodox liberal capitalism, is worth it and/or has a chance to survive in the twenty-first century global economy. We need a more neutral approach, one that does not take for granted that liberal capitalism (if such a thing really exists anywhere at all) is intrinsically superior to coordinated capitalism, or that European policymakers are truly coordinating capitalism according to their voters' and citizens' dominant values.

This is the standpoint from which this book analyses the European Union's Common Agricultural Policy. In addition to its intrinsic importance within the EU, an aspect that makes the CAP interesting for the broader debate on the European model is that its historical trajectory has eventually made it become a valuable contrast case. As we will see throughout the book, European agriculture during the last quarter century has experienced an unquestionable turn towards the market. Deregulation has been a key element of the reform agenda that started to be implemented in the 1990s and goes on to the present day. Present-day CAP is thus more market-oriented than the original CAP of the 1960s. And, yet, this market turn has been much more modest than in the rest of economic sectors. In manufacturing, for instance, the economic crisis of the 1970s triggered a response that eventually involved the discontinuation of most of the vertical, sector-level policies that national European governments had been applying until then. The EU itself, by means of its policies in search of a transnational market free of distortions to competition, contributed to dismantling these national policies without substituting them with an alternative, European-level industrial policy. Getting back to another important example, the financial sector has also gone through substantial deregulation – initially as a result of national policy agendas that were at a later stage strengthened and amplified at the EU level. In comparison, agriculture has been different, and this gives us a promising area in which to explore the pros and cons of Europe's coordinated capitalism.

Praising the "European model of agriculture"

The main arguments supporting European-style coordinated capitalism for agriculture have been carefully elaborated by the European Commission during more than half a century of CAP history. All of them share common ground: for the Commission, the CAP provides nonmarket mechanisms in order to deal with the social, environmental and territorial problems caused by agrarian change. Consequently, the argument continues, we are better off with the European institutions coordinating agriculture and rural society than leaving these fully exposed to the impersonal decisions stemming from completely free markets. Thanks to the CAP, European agriculture would be embedded in a set of values that would not be satisfactorily represented under a more market-oriented, liberal version of capitalism.

What are those values? During the CAP's first era, from its implementation in the 1960s to the 1980s, the Commission's main argument focused on social justice. Free markets would create too large a gap between farmers' income and that of the rest of the citizens. All over Europe, farmers were much less productive and had an income that was well below their respective national average. Farmers were the occupational group with the highest risk of falling below national poverty lines. That is where a policy such as the CAP, set to support farm income and bring farmers' income closer to the rest of citizens, would come in.

It is true that officially the original CAP had a number of additional objectives. The foundational Treaty of Rome of 1957, for instance, also made reference to increasing agricultural productivity, stabilizing agricultural markets, securing food availability, and guaranteeing reasonable food prices for consumers. However, as was admitted even by the EU justice system early on, these objectives were partly contradictory to one another, and the CAP could not be expected to achieve all of them simultaneously and fully (Cardwell 2004: 20). A detailed analysis of the political bargaining that defined the original CAP reveals that it was the farm income problem that all participants in the policy process rapidly identified as the chief objective (Knudsen 2009a).

The positioning of the CAP as a policy for farm income support has actually persisted to the present day. The Commission presents the CAP as an agricultural application of the principles and values that inspire European-style coordinated capitalism. One of the identifying marks of European capitalism has been the construction of a strong welfare state by means of which citizens get access to wide-ranging health and educational services, as well as social protection. Social protection, in particular, has been oriented towards increasing the income levels and capabilities of those citizens and social groups that are more vulnerable; for instance, retirement pensions for the elderly and unemployment benefits for the unemployed. The CAP would then be an EU-level complement to the conventional social protection instruments existing at the national level. In the expression coined by political scientist Adam Sheingate (2001) for this sort of policies, the CAP could be seen as an "agricultural welfare state". As the history of the CAP moved forward, the trend towards farmer ageing (and the consequent unlikelihood that low-income farmers can fluidly transition to other sectors in the economy) has probably reinforced this parallelism between national policies for social protection and the CAP.

During the last quarter century, the traditional argument in terms of social justice has been joined by a newer one that presents the CAP as beneficial not only for farmers but also for the rest of society (Knudsen 2009b; European Commission 2012; Allons and Zwaan 2016). This has substantially widened the range of values represented by the CAP (Knudsen 2009b: 291–299), in particular by incorporating the environment and rural development. A third dimension, food security, has been on the rise within EU discourse (Cardwell 2004: 265–285), but since it is of little relevance in terms of the actual measures making up the CAP we will leave it aside.

In environmental terms, the Commission stresses the benefits that maintaining farming all across Europe brings to society as a whole. Agrarian landscapes, such as we perceive and value them, are not really natural, but result from the cultivation and livestock-rearing practices developed by generations of previous farmers. Supporting farmers would be a way of preserving this eco-cultural patrimony and preventing its degradation. Not allowing massive abandonment of arable and pasture lands could also prevent scrub and weeds from spreading chaotically. Even the risk of forest fires could be mitigated as a result of these measures. Other contributions of the CAP to environmental protection would be the promotion of crop diversification, afforestation and organic agriculture. The message is clear: Europe faces the challenge of transitioning towards a sustainable economy, and the CAP is part of the solution.

The idea that it is society as a whole, and not just the farming community, that benefits from the CAP has been elaborated also in the area of rural development. One of the major threats to European territorial cohesion is the depopulation of rural areas, which in some parts of the Union has become truly extreme. The Commission argues that supporting farmers attaches population to the rural territory: in the absence of the CAP, the abandonment of farms would have gone much further than it already has. Moreover, supporting farmers may be a way of stimulating the development of local food-processing industries and other economic activities that also make a contribution to affixing population to rural areas.

These newer arguments crystallized into the term "European model of agriculture" that was popularized by the Commission in the 1990s (Cardwell 2004). By means of this term, the Commission wanted to position the CAP within the broader European tradition of a social market economy, as opposed to the more liberal orientation of American capitalism. The Commission had the chance to capitalize on the OECD's elaboration of the notion of agriculture as a "multifunctional" activity. According to this, farmers not only produce food. As a collateral effect, they also produce environmental and territorial services. Free markets, however, do not provide any remuneration for these services. Therefore, public policy should compensate farmers for providing them. Towards the end of the millennium, and partly thanks to the intellectual support provided by the OECD, European commissioner for Agriculture, Franz Fischler, was able to argue that

> the fundamental difference between the European model and that of our major competitors lies in the multifunctional nature of Europe's agriculture and the part it plays in the economy and the environment, in society and in preserving the landscape, whence the need to maintain farming throughout Europe and to safeguard farmers' incomes.
>
> *(cf. Cardwell 2004: 94)*

In the words of the European Parliament in the 1990s, what the European institutions were doing was to define a "renewed contract between agriculture and society" (Cardwell 2004: 413).

During the early years of the new millennium, European institutions extensively used the notion of a "European model of agriculture" and, still today, we can find frequent allusions to it among policymakers and stakeholders (Lovec 2016: 151). But, even though the term was new, the idea behind it had been part of the Commission's discourse from the very start of the CAP. Mistrust in liberal agrarian capitalism, in which the market would be the only coordinator of the economy, was explicit in the 1960s already. The comparison with an essentially different US model appeared later, but by the 1980s had become explicit as well (Cardwell 2004: 1–2, 37). In sum, pro-CAP arguments have been based on values which – as in the cases of social justice, environmental protection and territorial cohesion – the Commission believes to be better represented by some sort of coordinated capitalism than by liberal capitalism.

It is important to note that European public opinion has been generally sympathetic to these values and to the CAP as an expression of them (Cardwell 2004: 405–406). Time and again, citizens in the Commission's Eurobarometer believe that agriculture and rural areas are important for the future of Europe and that, in general terms, the CAP is performing reasonably well. If in the 1980s almost half of Europeans made a positive assessment of the CAP as opposed to less than 20 per cent who made a negative assessment (Commission of the European Communities 1988: VIII), the latest survey (conducted in 2017) shows Europeans to be even more supportive, with the proportion of those believing that the CAP is meeting its objectives ranging between 52 and 72 per cent (European Commission 2018: 11). The idea that the CAP benefits society as a whole and not just farmers is endorsed by more than 60 per cent of Europeans, which represents more than three out of every four citizens who declare to have an opinion on the issue (European

TABLE 1.1 Eurobarometer results on the CAP budget (%)

	Question: "Over the next ten years would you like to see an increase, decrease or no change in EU financial support to farmers?"			
	Increase	No change	Decrease	Don't know
1987[a]	27	26	22	25
2007	29	29	18	24
2017	44	29	12	15

Sources: Commission of the European Communities (1988: V); European Commission (2018: 17).
Note: [a] Adapted from the question "Do you think that in your country and in the rest of the European Community, the public authorities spend too much money on agriculture, not enough money or about the right amount?"

Commission 2018: 14). In fact, those who would rather see CAP's budget reduced are a tiny minority, while the preference for seeing that budget increased has come to be clearly dominant (Table 1.1).

Neoclassical economics against the CAP

Independent researchers are not so supportive of the CAP. Actually, much of the academic discourse on the CAP has always been blatantly critical. Critics not only dispute the validity of the justifications presented in the previous section, but also highlight the serious costs and dysfunctionalities brought about by this policy. For critics the CAP is like the creature that Victor Frankenstein brings to life in Mary Shelley's novel: a chaotic, incoherent mix of public policy instruments that has eventually assumed a life of its own and is beyond control by its very designers. The result is that the "monster" is loose and causing harm across the world, and not just in Europe. Some critics think that the CAP therefore needs very profound reforms, and others think that we would be better off without it at all, so that farmers and farming are liberated from the regulations designed in Brussels.

Economists, especially those affiliated with the intellectual tradition of neoclassical economics, have panned the CAP right from the beginning. Most of them believe that we would have been better off without the CAP. To begin with, European citizens would have saved a lot of money, since the CAP has always absorbed an utterly disproportionate share of the EU budget (and continues to do so). Or, at the least, this money could have been allocated to policies with more tangible benefits for European society as a whole. Moreover, consumers would have saved even more money, as they would have had free access to imported foodstuffs with a lower price than that of European products. The core problem is one of inefficiency: the estimations made by neoclassical economists concur that the costs borne by taxpayers and consumers have been larger than the benefits transferred to farmers. In other words, it is not that the CAP redistributes resources from some citizens to others, but the fact that in doing so resources are lost and aggregate welfare diminishes (Tracy 1989; Gardner 1996; Andreosso-O'Calaghan 2003; Anderson 2009).

Alongside allocative inefficiency, the CAP could also have provoked negative distortions over time. The CAP would have made Europe maintain too large a number of farmers and too high a level of agricultural production. If the EU had let markets work freely, more farms would have been closed, more arable land would have been abandoned and a greater reduction in livestock numbers would have taken place, but this would not have been any tragedy. It would have been merely a structural adjustment that, as the cases of other sectors (i.e. heavy industry, mining) show, would have allowed Europe to be more efficient, focusing its efforts on those activities in which we are truly competitive. If the negative impact of the CAP has not been larger, the argument goes on to say, is simply because this policy has been lucky enough to coincide with an era of rapid growth in Europe's nonfarm economy (Eichengreen 2007: 195; Josling 2009: 162–163; Houpt et al. 2010).

In terms of the underlying theoretical debate, neoclassical economists are close to the notion of liberal capitalism and tend to prefer that the adjustments derived from economic change take place primarily through the market. Their criticism also extends beyond European borders, arguing that the CAP provokes unfortunate distortions in international markets and hampers the economic development of the global South. Many of the households living in extreme poverty in the South are peasant households or are somehow connected to agricultural livelihoods, but by protecting European farmers, the EU would be depriving these households of opportunities to export to the European market. Making our market more open to food imports would be negative for our farmers, but positive for the (much needier) farmers in the global South. Dismantling the commercial fortress Europe would have become would provide opportunities for faster economic growth in the developing countries. In many of these countries, the nonfarm economy is so weak that agricultural exports would actually be the most feasible way to achieve economic development and poverty reduction, but the EU is blocking them.

There is more: with its long history of subsidies to exports, the EU has also harmed the interests of third countries – nonmembers of the EU – in another way. Subsidising Europeans who export agricultural products implies unfair trade competition, as our products are dumped into the markets of third countries at prices lower than their real cost. European policy would thus contribute to distorting the structure of relative prices prevailing in the South, draining material and human resources from domestic agricultures.

Some neoclassical economists have made estimations of the economic harm that the CAP causes to the global South and have reached the conclusion that this harm outweighs by far the amount of money allocated by the EU and its member states to development cooperation (Andreosso-O'Calaghan 2003: 227). Especially from the 1990s onwards, the EU has emerged as the main actor in the area of international development cooperation: it makes an effort in official development aid that is much greater than that of the United States or Japan, and it leads the international agenda for standardization and progress in cooperation policy. However, according to this line of criticism, all these efforts do not compensate for the negative impact of the CAP on developing countries. There would be no better pro-development policy than dismantling the distortions to international agricultural trade.

The overall assessment that historians make is strongly influenced by this set of arguments. This is very clear in, for instance, Giovanni Federico's explicitly neo-classical analysis, which takes as a starting point what he calls "a reminder of Econ 101" (that is, the first-year, introductory course to neoclassical microeconomics in English-speaking countries) and its main message: "Why state intervention is (usually) bad" (Federico 2009: 58). For Federico, the CAP was the worst agricultural policy in the world during the second half of the twentieth century and, without a doubt, "a liberal policy seems more preferable by far" (Federico 2011: 142). But historians with other sympathies are also very critical of the waste of resources and the distortions provoked by the CAP. For instance, a recognized social democrat historian such as Tony Judt (2005: 306, 723) considers it an "absurd […] set of policies" that has absorbed "hugely disproportionate sums of money", with "perverse consequences" unprecedented among modern agricultural policies. In other words, historians whose underlying ideal is not necessarily liberal capitalism have also been highly critical of the CAP (see also Brassley 1997; Béaur 2003; or Patel 2009).

However, these historians are far more comfortable analysing the CAP that was born in the 1960s than the reformed versions of it that have taken shape from the 1990s onwards. Federico barely takes notice of these reforms, which he argues did not bring about any substantial changes. Eichengreen (2007: 333) also sees the reforms as an opportunity missed for the EU to cut inefficient public support to farmers.

What this implies is that the historians influenced by neoclassical economics have not yet absorbed the recent evolution of research by neoclassical economists. Neoclassical economists may not have changed their minds substantially, but there has been a renewal in their research agenda: researchers have abandoned wholesale criticism and have embraced reflection about what the second-best option may be – that is, how to reform the CAP in order to make it better (Tracy 1989: 333). If the quantity of support provided by the EU to its farmers must be maintained for political reasons, economists can at least reflect on how to improve the quality of that support (in the terms of Federico 2009: 269–270). For most of the farmers, that would entail basically substituting the original instruments of the CAP, based on market intervention, with direct subsidies to farmers, which would have a lower impact on resource allocation efficiency (Hubbard and Ritson 1997; Swinnen 2018). Inasmuch as this is precisely what the reforms of the 1990s and 2000s did, neoclassical economists have had the chance to reposition themselves more optimistically, arguing that "[although] considerable distortion in Western European agriculture still exists, the path to reducing that distortion is opening up" (Josling 2009: 171; see also Anderson 2016: xxi).

Furthermore, from the 1990s onwards neoclassical economists began to be more receptive than usual to the identification of market failures that would justify some of the public support given to European farmers. In a way, the European Commission's new discourse on the multifunctionality of agriculture and the new social contract between farmers and society lent itself reasonably well to being framed in terms of neoclassical economic theory. A case could be made for maintaining a dense network of farms all across the European Union, so that society as a whole would benefit in environmental and cultural terms. Using neoclassical concepts, it could be argued that farmers produced not only food, but also relevant public goods related to the environment, the territory and culture. Since the market did not provide remuneration for the production of these public goods, a public policy that supported farmers was necessary in order to reach the social optimum. Economists such as Alan Buckwell were actually influential in the reorientation of the European Commission's discourse towards multifunctionality and the "European model of agriculture" (Koning 2017: Chapter 7).

This does not mean that neoclassical economists have become unanimous and unconditional supporters of the reformed CAP of the last quarter century. For some, the turn towards multifunctionality has been little more than a dishonest rhetorical manoeuvre meant to provide a new justification for the same old protectionism (Jones 2002). And for many others, perhaps a majority, CAP reforms have not yet been able to construct a sufficiently solid link between agricultural subsidies and the provision of environmental and territorial public goods by farmers. In their opinion, there is a large gap between the new justifications surrounding the CAP and actual reality (Cuhna and Swinbank 2011). All in all, and nevertheless, neoclassical economic discourse has moved to more constructive terrain than that of merely bashing the CAP. It is likely that most neoclassical economists still take liberal capitalism as their first choice, but they are becoming increasingly involved in practical reflection about how to improve coordinated capitalism.

Intellectual life outside "Econ 101"

The criticisms presented in the previous section have been at the forefront of the academic debate for a long time. There have been some who, such as World Bank economist Michael Atkin, have even written that "the CAP really has no defenders on an intellectual level" (cf. Cunha and Swinbank 2011: 201n.). However, this is a major exaggeration because, in spite of some economists not being entirely aware of it, there is intellectual life outside "Econ 101". When it comes to the CAP, this intellectual life has developed through other schools of economic thought and other social sciences, including history.

Agricultural economists in continental Europe, for instance, have traditionally taken a more moderate stand on the CAP. For much of our period, their education has been less influenced by the neoclassical paradigm than that of their English-speaking peers, so that they have been less worried about allocative efficiency and more about the social and structural context. As British economist Michael Tracy

(1989: x) commented with genuine surprise in the 1980s, his French colleagues hardly ever criticized agricultural policies.

Louis Malassis (1997: 303–306), perhaps the most prominent agricultural economist in France during the decades after the Second World War, indeed makes a more benevolent assessment of the CAP. According to Malassis, this policy would have reached almost all of its objectives. The CAP would have supported the modernization of Europe's agriculture and the rapid rise that took place in farmers' productivity. It would have also guaranteed a sufficient food supply, making it possible for Europeans to comfortably meet their needs. Perhaps CAP's main shortcoming would have been not being able to close the income gap between farmers and the rest of society. All in all, and reformulating the argument in terms of the debate on varieties of capitalism, for Malassis the CAP would have been a reasonably effective policy when it came to coordinating the interests of producers and consumers at a time of accelerated change in agriculture and in Europe's economy and society as a whole.

Sociologists have also tended to take as a starting point a less critical predisposition towards the CAP and coordinated capitalism. For Niek Koning (2017: Chapters 4 and 6), for instance, the making of the CAP has to be seen within a longer historical cycle that would have started in the late nineteenth century and during which Europe implemented policies that favoured a path of agricultural modernization based on family farms (see also Gallego 2007; Chang 2009; Moser and Varley 2013). In his opinion, had European governments chosen not to intervene, the result would have been worse, not only in terms of social cohesion, but probably also in terms of long-run output trends. The case of much of Latin America and Africa, where governments did not implement that sort of policy during the decades after the Second World War, would suggest so. Even though Koning holds a critical position on the recent evolution of the CAP (as we will see later), his ideal – in no small measure realized during twentieth-century European history – remains undoubtedly some sort of coordinated agrarian capitalism.

This view has spread among economic historians much less than that of an inefficient, distorting policy (but see an exception in Zamagni 2017: Chapter 15). In political history, however, a new image of the CAP's past, one very different from that inspired by "Econ 101", is taking shape. Ann-Christina L. Knudsen (2009a, 2009b), in particular, has sought to shift the debate from the field of efficiency, so dear to neoclassical economists, to the field of equality, one of the traditional feuds of those supporting coordinated capitalism. For Knudsen, the analysis of the CAP has to be positioned within the wider context of the expansion of Western European welfare states after 1945. It is pointless to see the CAP exclusively or primarily in terms of efficiency because first and foremost it was "a redistributive policy with an objective not at all different from the social transfer policies of welfare states" (Knudsen 2009a: 3).

Once the playing field was set in terms of equality, Knudsen (2009a: 267–275) seems to admit the existence of more than a few problems on the CAP's balance sheet. In her view, the original CAP repeated the mistake that was already being made in the pre-existing national policies of farm-income support: to take for granted that there was a strong link between farm income and agricultural prices and, as a result, to design an allegedly universal solution to the farm-income problem through the manipulation of agricultural prices. This eventually implied that the CAP benefited the largest, most efficient farmers the most and was unable to close the income gap between farmers and the rest of society. However, and in spite of it all, Knudsen (2009a: 317) explicitly moves away from the fierce criticism raised by neoclassical economists: quoting Giovanni Federico for her own purposes, she suggests that it was a success that European agriculture managed to easily ensure the feeding of the Europeans, while she admits having developed the "utmost fascination with the seriousness of the CAP as a political construction".

These moderately positive views of the CAP have, however, evolved in a critical direction in the last few decades. Paradoxically, as neoclassical economists were abandoning wholesale criticism for a reformist discourse, the messages coming from outside "Econ 101" were turning sour. Perhaps sociology and geography, two disciplines whose agricultural specialities are separated by blurred frontiers, provide the best illustration.

For sociologists and geographers, the starting point had never been the superiority of liberal capitalism, so it was not necessary to vindicate non-market coordination in terms of tightly defined exceptions to the general rule. The reorientation of the Commission's discourse towards multifunctionality and the European model of agriculture in the 1990s actually widened the range of political values that CAP-coordinated capitalism could be expected to incorporate in a more reliable way than could an alternative, deregulated capitalism. As was the case with economists, some sociologists were even influential at giving shape to the Commission's new ideas. In France, in particular, Bertrand Hervieu (1996) usefully imagined *Les champs du futur* (The fields of the future) from the standpoint of a new social contract between farmers and the rest of society. Under this new contract, farmers would receive a fair remuneration for the whole scope of the social functions they were performing, not only food production, but also non-market functions such as preserving the environment and favouring territorial cohesion. Geographers, on their part, had the chance to position the new CAP within the constellation of a "post-productivist" transition in which intensification, concentration and specialization would be giving way to extensive farming, geographical dispersion and output diversification (Ilbery and Bowler 1998). Sociologists and geographers alike developed an enthusiastic interest in studying the effects of the new European policies for rural development.

And yet, precisely at the time when their incorporation into a reformist agenda shared with economists seemed more feasible, sociologists and geographers began to produce ever more-disenchanted analyses. Soon the sensation that actual reality was far from the promise of the "European model of agriculture" – and that the latter was basically a large list of unfulfilled objectives – began to spread (Buller 2001). The multifunctionality discourse increasingly came to be seen as merely that: a discourse, one that was more effective at renewing the legitimacy of the CAP than the CAP itself (Lovec 2016). For instance, there has been repeated criticism that there is a large distance between the ideal of social justice that apparently inspires the CAP and the actual distribution of CAP subsidies – distribution that is strongly skewed in favour of the largest landowners (Segrelles 2017). This distance between the ideal and the actual was probably more painful for sociologists and geographers – well predisposed to the ideal of coordinated capitalism – than for neoclassical economists, who had never expected much from it anyway.

Moreover, the discourse outside "Econ 101" has turned even more sour as the political environment surrounding the CAP has become that of an increasingly deregulated global economy. As has been argued by Niek Koning (2017: Chapter 7) or Philip McMichael (2013), the CAP becomes problematic, especially from the moment when the political environment in which it played a part, the welfare state, vanishes. It is true that by then the CAP already had a history of negative impacts on the development of the global South, especially when it came to subsidizing exports of European surpluses entering the markets of poorer countries and therefore weakening their domestic agri-food systems. But the problem would have become much more serious from the moment (around the 1980s) the developed countries started to orient the GATT (General Agreement on Tariffs and Trade) and the World Trade Organization towards the liberalization of international agricultural markets. The outcome would have been strikingly asymmetrical: while the countries from the South were forced to dismantle their trade barriers in relation to countries from the North, the latter were able to retain most of their agricultural subsidy programmes after having implemented "pseudo-liberalizing" reforms such as the one inspired by the EU–OECD notion of multifunctionality. As a result, the CAP would basically go on subsidizing European farmers at the expense of farmers in the global South. Since agri-food markets are much more integrated today than they were in the decades after the Second World War (in large measure, precisely because of the neoliberal policies promoted by the GATT and the WTO), the impact of policies such as the CAP on the global South would have been particularly negative in the present time (McMichael 2013: 6, 34–35, 52, 77; see also Magnan 2012).

According to this line of analysis, the problem for the global South is not the agri-exporting opportunity missed, but the disarticulation of local agricultural systems that follows the dumping of European surpluses. This would make the South increasingly vulnerable to price fluctuations that take place in an international market over which their own governments lack any control. Sudden spikes in international agricultural prices would then menace food security in much of the developing world. A number of governmental and non-governmental organizations have accepted this analysis and have subsequently criticized the incoherence of EU policies (Fritz 2012; Koning 2017: Chapter 7). In the words of Olivier de Schutter, when he was the United Nations Special Rapporteur on the right to food, "The CAP is a 50-billion-euro contradiction with respect to the EU's commitment of helping agriculture in the developing world to recover" (cf. Fritz 2012: 47).

It is true that the great change vindicated by the sociologists and geographers in this vein has less to do with policies such as the CAP themselves than with the lack of room for manoeuvring that poor countries have when it comes to implementing policies that differ from neoliberalism. For McMichael (2013: 57), poor countries should be able to defend their frontiers from imported food and organize their agricultural systems in accordance with the principles of food sovereignty. For Koning (2017), quantitative controls should be implemented in order to stabilize international markets, which would lead to something close to what we could call (in the terms used in this book) coordinated agrarian capitalism on a global scale. It is remarkable, nonetheless, that more and more researchers in the world outside "Econ 101", without any a priori bias against the notion of coordinated capitalism, have come to see the CAP in a negative light.

Conclusion

The debate on varieties of capitalism and the European model casts a long shadow on the more specific debate on the CAP. When the EU institutions defend the CAP, they position it within the continental European tradition of coordinated capitalism, emphasizing its capacity to embody social, environmental and territorial values more effectively than would be the case under a more market-oriented variety of capitalism. The support that public opinion seems to give to the CAP does not come so much from detailed knowledge of its practice as from a broader backing of the values of coordinated agrarian capitalism. The divergent opinions of academic researchers are also substantially influenced by their more-general opinions on coordinated versus liberal capitalism. Most economists belong to the neoclassical school, which makes them attach much importance to efficiency in resource allocation and be more favourably predisposed towards liberal capitalism (with only exceptional public intervention in order to correct a small number of well-defined market failures). Outside the world of neoclassical economics, conversely, the introduction of evaluation dimensions other than allocative efficiency is more common, and the analysis takes place in a framework that is less hostile to the CAP.

Yet, these divergent orientations have not predetermined the course of the debate. In fact, the debate has evolved substantially through time, reflecting (at least partly) the changes that have taken place in the CAP itself and in the discourse held by the European Commission in order to justify the CAP. During an early stage, between the 1960s and the 1990s, the European Commission positioned the CAP as a welfare state policy with the chief objective being to increase farmers' incomes. Most economists were highly critical of this policy, which today historians who are influenced by neoclassical economics portray as a textbook example of why the state should not intervene in a market economy. However, over the last three decades the arguments in the debate have gone through substantial renewal. In parallel to successive reforms in the CAP, the Commission has come to position this policy in terms of not only social justice, but also environmental protection and territorial cohesion. In fact, the Commission eventually coined the notion of a "European model of agriculture" in order to make explicit a number of political values that until then had underpinned the CAP in a more implicit way. These changes in the CAP, for their part, have had a substantial impact on academic debates in the various disciplines. Economists remain unenthusiastic about the CAP, but are reasonably satisfied with the direction of the reforms that have taken place in the last few decades. Sociologists and geographers, on the other hand, have moved from a favourable predisposition towards coordinated capitalism to increasing hostility towards the CAP.

An important implication is that we need to frame the debate on the CAP in its historical dimension. The evolution of the debate that has been reviewed in this chapter suggests the existence of differentiated stages and critical turning points. The next chapter describes what the CAP was about in each of these stages. In addition, we also need to formulate the debate on the CAP within the field defined by the broader debate on the European model and the varieties of capitalism. As we have seen in this chapter, the terms of the debate should not take for granted that the EU's discourse on a distinctively European model is necessarily in accordance with reality, nor that coordinated capitalisms are exceptions to the rule of a supposedly triumphant global liberal capitalism. The description of the CAP that follows in Chapter 2 will be useful in order to compare the CAP to the agricultural policies of other countries and regions and assess whether this policy actually embodies a distinctively European model of agriculture.

References

Alesina, A. and Giavazzi, F. 2006. *The future of Europe: Reform or decline*. Cambridge, MA: MIT Press.

Allons, G. and Zwaan, P. 2016. "New wine in different bottles: Negotiating and selling the CAP post-2013 reform". *Sociologia Ruralis* 56 (3): 349–370.

Anderson, K. 2009. "Five decades of distortions to agricultural incentives". In *Distortions to agricultural incentives: A global perspective, 1955–2007*, ed. K. Anderson, 3–64. Washington, DC: World Bank and Palgrave Macmillan.

Anderson, K. 2016. *Agricultural trade, policy reforms, and global food security*. New York: Palgrave Macmillan.

Andreosso-O'Callaghan, B. 2003. *The economics of European agriculture*. Basingstoke: Palgrave Macmillan.

Béaur, G. 2003. "Agricultural policy". In *The Oxford encyclopedia of economic history*, ed. J. Mokyr, 32–36. New York: Oxford University Press.

Boyer, R. 2005. "How and why capitalisms differ". *Economy and Society* 34 (4): 509–557.

Brassley, P. 1997. *Agricultural economics and the CAP: An introduction*. Oxford: Blackwell.

Buller, H. 2001. "Is this the European model?". In *Agricultural transformation, food and environment: Perspectives on European rural policy and planning*, eds. H. Buller and K. Hoggart, 1–8. Aldershot: Ashgate.

Cardwell, M. 2004. *The European model of agriculture*. Oxford: Oxford University Press.

Chang, H.-J. 2009. "Rethinking public policy in agriculture: Lessons from history, distant and recent". *Journal of Peasant Studies* 36 (3): 477–515.

Commission of the European Communities. 1988. *Eurobarometer – Europeans and their agriculture*. Luxembourg: Directorate-General Information, Communication, Culture.

Cunha, A. and Swinbank, A. 2011. *An inside view of the CAP reform process: Explaining the MacSharry, Agenda 2000, and Fischler reforms*. Oxford: Oxford University Press.

Eichengreen, B. 2007. *The European economy since 1945: Coordinated capitalism and beyond*. Princeton: Princeton University Press.

European Commission. 2012. *The Common Agricultural Policy: A story to be continued*. Luxembourg: Office for Official Publications of the European Communities.

European Commission. 2018. *Special Eurobarometer 473: Europeans, agriculture and the CAP*. Luxembourg: Office for Official Publications of the European Communities.

Federico, G. 2009. "Was the CAP the worst agricultural policy of the 20th century?". In *Fertile ground for Europe? The history of European integration and the Common Agricultural Policy since 1945*, ed. K. K. Patel, 257–271. Baden-Baden: Nomos.

Federico, G. 2011. *Breve historia económica de la agricultura*. Zaragoza: Prensas Universitarias de Zaragoza and Institución Fernando el Católico.

Freeman, C. 1995. "The 'National System of Innovation' in historical perspective". *Cambridge Journal of Economics* 19 (1): 5–24.

Fritz, T. 2012. *Globalizar el hambre: impactos de la Política Agrícola Común (PAC) y de las políticas comerciales de la UE en la soberanía alimentaria y los países del Sur*. Madrid: ACSUR-Las Segovias, Ecologistas en Acción, Plataforma 2015, Plataforma Rural, Veterinarios sin Fronteras and Asociación Trashumancia y Naturaleza.

Gallego, D. 2007. *Más allá de la economía de mercado: los condicionantes históricos del desarrollo económico*. Madrid: Marcial Pons.

Gardner, B. 1996. *European agriculture: Policies, production and trade*. London: Routledge.

Hall, P. A. and Soskice, D. 2001. "An introduction to varieties of capitalism". In *Varieties of capitalism: the institutional foundations of comparative advantage*, eds. P. A. Hall and D. Soskice, 1–68. Oxford: Oxford University Press.

Hervieu, B. 1996. *Los campos del futuro*. Madrid: Ministerio de Agricultura, Pesca y Alimentación.

Houpt, S., Lains, P., and Schön, L. 2010. "Sectoral developments". In *The Cambridge economic history of modern Europe, vol. 2: 1870–2000*, eds. K. H. O'Rourke and S. Broadberry, 333–359. Cambridge: Cambridge University Press.

Hubbard, L. and Ritson, C. 1997. "Reform of the CAP: From Mansholt to MacSharry". In *The Common Agricultural Policy*, eds. C. Ritson and D. R. Harvey, 81–94. Wallingford: CAB International.

Ilbery, B. and Bowler, I. 1998. "From agricultural productivism to post-productivism". In *The geography of rural change*, ed. B. Ilbery, 57–84. Essex: Longman.

Jones, E. 2002. *The record of global economic development*. Cheltenham: Edward Elgar.

Josling, T. 2009. "Western Europe". In *Distortions to agricultural incentives: A global perspective, 1955–2007*, ed. K. Anderson, 115–176. Washington, DC: World Bank and Palgrave Macmillan.

Judt, T. 2005. *Postwar: A history of Europe since 1945*. London: Penguin.

Knudsen, A.-C. L. 2009a. *Farmers on welfare: The making of Europe's Common Agricultural Policy*. Ithaca, NY: Cornell University Press.

Knudsen, A.-C. L. 2009b. "Ideas, welfare, and values. Framing the Common Agricultural Policy in the 1960s". In *Fertile ground for Europe? The history of European integration and the Common Agricultural Policy since 1945*, ed. K. K. Patel, 61–78. Baden-Baden: Nomos.

Koning, N. 2017. *Food security, agricultural policies and economic growth: Long-term dynamics in the past, present and future*. London: Routledge.

Lovec, M. 2016. *The European Union's Common Agricultural Policy reforms*. London: Palgrave Macmillan.

McMichael, P. 2013. *Food regimes and agrarian questions*. Winnipeg: Fernwood.

Magnan, A. 2012. "Food regimes". In *Oxford handbook of food history*, ed. J. M. Pilcher, 370–388. New York: Oxford University Press.

Malassis, L. 1997. *Les trois âges de l'alimentaire. Essai sur une histoire sociale de l'alimentation et de l'agriculture, II: L'âge agro-industriel*. Paris: Cujas.

Mazzucato, M. 2013. *The entrepreneurial state: Debunking public vs. private sector myths*. London: Anthem.

Moser, P. and Varley, T. 2013. "The state and agricultural modernisation in the nineteenth and twentieth centuries in Europe". In *Integration through subordination: The politics of agricultural modernisation in industrial Europe*, eds. P. Moser and T. Varley, 13–39. Turnhout: Brepols.

Patel, K. K. 2009. "The history of European integration and the Common Agricultural Policy: An introduction". In *Fertile ground for Europe? The history of European integration and the Common Agricultural Policy since 1945*, ed. K. K. Patel, 7–23. Baden-Baden: Nomos.

Sapir, A., Aghion, P., Bertola, G., Hellwig, M., Pisani-Ferry, J., Rosati, D., Viñals, J., Wallace, H., Buti, M., Nava, M., and Smith, P. M. 2004. *An agenda for a growing Europe: The Sapir report*. Oxford: Oxford University Press.

Segrelles, J. A. 2017. "Las ayudas agrarias y sus repercusiones sobre la agricultura familiar en la última reforma de la Política Agraria Común (2014–2020) de la Unión Europea: ¿cambiar para que todo siga igual?". *Boletín de la Asociación de Geógrafos Españoles* 74: 161–183.

Sheingate, A. D. 2001. *The rise of the agricultural welfare state: Institutions and interest group power in the United States, France, and Japan*. Princeton: Princeton University Press.

Swinnen, J. 2018. *The political economy of agricultural and food policies*. New York: Palgrave Macmillan.

Tooze, A. 2018. *Crashed: How a decade of financial crises changed the world*. New York: Penguin.

Tracy, M. 1989. *Government and agriculture in Western Europe, 1880–1988*. New York: New York University Press.

Zamagni, V. 2017. *An economic history of Europe since 1700*. Newcastle upon Tyne: Agenda.

2

WHAT IS THE CAP ABOUT?

In the book that the European Commission published on the occasion of the CAP's fiftieth anniversary, is the statement that "This is the story of a dynamic partnership between farmers and Europe" (European Commission 2012: 1). Later we will have the chance to evaluate the merits of this partnership, but for the moment what interests us most is the word "dynamic": the CAP has gone through substantial transformations from the 1960s to the present. The original CAP was relatively stable until the 1980s, but substantial reforms have taken place over the last quarter century. While this author was completing the present book in November 2019, an ongoing round of negotiations was defining a new reform that would be implemented in 2021 (or, perhaps more feasibly, around 2023).

This chapter describes the main elements of the CAP and their historical evolution as a necessary context for further analysis. This description will also allow us to assess the degree up to which we can talk of a distinctively European model of agriculture and, if there is one, what its singularity is. As the broader debate on varieties of capitalism and the European model shows, it is important to tackle the issue from the viewpoint of the actually existing policies, rather than from the viewpoint of discourses and values.

This chapter is organized in five sections. The first presents the concepts upon which our description will be based. The second and third sections apply said concepts to the two main eras in the history of the CAP: before and after 1992. Before 1992, as the second section shows, the main element of the CAP was public intervention in agricultural markets. In contrast, after 1992 (as the third section shows) the CAP transitioned to paying subsidies to farmers. The fourth and fifth sections complete this description. The fourth section describes the tension between the common, supranational character of the CAP and trends towards "re-nationalization", while the fifth section situates the CAP within the bigger picture of agricultural policies in other parts of the world.

Agricultural policy paradigms

The evolution of the CAP is commonly described in a chronological way, moving the reader from one turning point to the next, from the creation of the CAP to later reforms and changes. No doubt this is a useful way of organizing the information and suggesting to the reader the existence of a path-dependent process in the evolution of the policy over time. One problem of this strictly chronological approach, though, is that it can obscure the way in which different turning points involve a sharp break in relation to the past or, conversely, continuity and minor adjustments.

As an alternative, in this chapter we use the concept "policy paradigm" coined by political scientist Peter Hall (1993). According to this concept, policies tend to cluster in paradigms that feature relative stability in their objectives, principles and mechanisms of implementation. Many changes in specific policies are merely adjustments and revisions undertaken within the prevailing paradigm. Other changes are, on the contrary, of a more radical nature and, when a number of them come together in time, they may lead to paradigm change. This is basically an application to the political sphere of philosopher of science Thomas Kuhn's paradigm thinking, a theoretical move that has also been made in economics by the evolutionary school (Freeman and Louçã 2001).

Depending on the criteria used to tell continuity from change, different researchers may obtain different results in terms of policy paradigm identification. In the case of the CAP, some have used a discursive criterion to conclude that there have been two paradigms in the history of the CAP: an original protectionist paradigm, followed from the 1990s onwards by a "liberal-multifunctional" paradigm (Lovec 2016: 27–28). This proposal highlights the radical nature of the changes taking place in the last few decades. Others have focused on the objectives and practice of the CAP to argue that no substantial rupture took place in the 1990s (Kay 2006: 90–103). According to this, there would have been only one policy paradigm during the history of CAP, and it would be characterized by the granting of public support to farmers and the need to frame the policy (and especially its economic dimension) within fragile and yet stable power balances among member states.

These proposals are interesting, but they probably miss what we should look at first when it comes to identifying policy paradigms: the policies that were actually implemented. In the case of agriculture, there are two major families of policies set to grant public support to farmers. The first are the policies of agricultural market intervention, which can affect prices, quantities or both. The list of policy options here is very long and ranges from the setting of minimum prices for agricultural products to public purchases of surplus agricultural production or protectionist trade barriers in relation to foreign farmers. As a matter of fact, all these options can be combined in different proportions and different ways in order to pursue the objective of making farm income higher than it would have been in a free-market situation.

This is an objective that can also be pursued by means of a second family of agricultural policies: direct payments to farmers. Here the possibilities are also many.

States can pay subsidies to all their farmers, but they can also define restrictive criteria that favour some farmers over others. These criteria, in turn, can also be very varied and may have to do with farmers' output specialization, the size of their farms, the environmental and/or territorial implications of their farming style, or their degree of orientation towards technological and marketing innovations.

Both types of agricultural policies provide farmers with public support, but they do so in essentially different ways. Market intervention subsidizes farmers implicitly, whereas direct payments do so explicitly. The cost of the implicit subsidies involved in market intervention is borne by consumers, who have to accept food prices higher than those that would have resulted from a free market, while the burden of direct payments is on the public budget and, therefore, on taxpayers.

The CAP is composed of a large number of policy instruments, which have been combined and recombined in changing ways through time. It is possible, however, to perceive a historical evolution in the dominant instrument. During its first thirty years (1962–1992), the CAP was mostly a market-intervention policy. Over the last quarter century, however, the CAP has become mostly a policy of direct farm subsidies. This discontinuity in the dominant instrument, which is in line with the already-noted discontinuity in policy discourse (Lovec 2016: 27–28), suggests the existence of two distinct policy paradigms in the history of the CAP.

The CAP as market intervention (1962–1992)

The original CAP, implemented during Dutch commissioner Sicco Mansholt's term, was a policy by means of which the European Economic Community (EEC) intervened strongly in the functioning of agricultural markets in order to support farm income. This intervention combined price and quantity instruments, as well as an internal and an external dimension (Tracy 1989: Chapters 12–15; Gardner 1996; Ackrill 2000; García Delgado and García Grande 2005; Kay 2006: 93–96).

Price intervention was mostly about the EEC setting minimum prices for agricultural products. In a free market, the prices of agricultural products would fluctuate according to shifts in supply and demand, but the EEC decided to set a lower limit to the fluctuation: the prices realized by farmers would not fall below some predetermined threshold. In order to be effective, this was joined by trade protectionism in relation to third countries. From the late nineteenth century onwards, it had become technically feasible for European countries to participate in global markets for the main agricultural products. The transport revolution implied by the introduction of railways and steamships had made it possible for farmers in America, Oceania and Russia, where land was abundant, to invade Europe's grain market and displace uncompetitive domestic farmers. However, most European governments (with the only major exception of Great Britain) had adopted protectionist policies that limited their farmers' exposure to international competition. The CAP unified these national trade policies within a common trade policy with common tariffs.

This allowed the EEC to exert remarkable control over the price levels prevailing in its domestic market. The common tariff implied an extra charge on the price of agricultural products from outside the EEC, so that they did not have the chance to access European consumers at a price lower than the minimum price set by the EEC for European farmers. In a way, trade relations with the outside were subordinated to the domestic objective of setting political prices on the inside. For practical matters, the key issue was fixing those political prices. For most products and conjunctures, a free market would have led to low prices through the pressure of international competition or the pressure of competition among European farmers themselves. By setting guaranteed minimum prices at levels that were higher than those of market equilibrium, the EEC made it possible for farmers to obtain a higher income for the sale of their produce.

But, in order to be effective, intervention via prices had to be complemented with some intervention via quantity. Otherwise, public intervention would risk making things worse for farmers, instead of better. Having the guarantee of high prices allowed them to sell their produce for more money, but would they really be able to find any buyers for their produce? Higher-than-equilibrium prices would perhaps imply a contraction in the demand for agricultural products, which would cause farmers a problem with overproduction. Additional policy instruments were needed in order to face this possible problem.

The first was so-called "intervention buying", by means of which the EEC committed to absorbing any surplus production by acting as a purchaser of last resort. If farmers were not able to sell all of their produce, the EEC would buy surplus production from them at a predetermined, remunerative price. More precisely, what happened in most cases is that the EEC would buy surplus production from processing industries and commercial intermediaries that had previously absorbed surplus agricultural production from farmers. For instance, the EEC would absorb the surplus milk produced by farmers by absorbing the surplus butter that dairy processors had produced with farmers' surplus milk. By offering these incentives to processors and traders, the EEC was able to provide farmers with a gloriously horizontal demand curve for their products: high prices would not contract demand (as would be the case in a free market), and demand would be potentially unlimited.

Another way of creating a horizontal demand for farmers was to divert their surplus production to other parts of the world. Instead of losing money with its purchases of surplus production (which at a later stage would usually be resold at a price not higher than around one third of intervention price), the EEC would subsidize those companies that were able to sell some of their output in other, non-EEC markets. Basically, this was a way of returning companies the money that they had previously used to pay artificially high prices to farmers. As a result, European processors would improve their international competitiveness and would be in a better position to export to non-EEC markets.

Finally, the European agricultural market could also be regulated by means of a third mechanism: instead of absorbing or diverting overproduction, the EEC could try to prevent it. The EEC had the option of implementing quantitative restrictions that would prevent or discourage farmers from producing too much. The most severe of these restrictions would be the introduction of farm-level output quotas, so that every farmer was assigned a maximum level of output beyond which they were not allowed to continue their operation. This is the instrument that the EEC would eventually implement in the dairy sector, but in general terms it was softer versions of the idea that prevailed. These included quantitative restrictions at sector level (rather than at the level of the individual farm) and output thresholds beyond which the EEC would stop acting as a buyer of last resort or would apply automatic reductions in guaranteed minimum prices.

Defined like this, as a system of farm support based on strong market intervention, the CAP did not go through major changes during its first thirty years of history. Perhaps the major change had to do with the proportions in which these different options of surplus management were combined. Originally, the main instrument was intervention buying, but export subsidies eventually came to be more important. Quantitative restrictions, on their part, did not play any role prior to the 1980s. Moreover, when they began to be applied, the EEC's preference for soft instruments implied that quantitative restrictions were always secondary in relation to intervention buying and export subsidies.

Another minor change was the introduction of a group of "structural" measures in the 1970s. These were active policies oriented towards improving farmers' competitiveness: subsidies for the introduction of technological innovations, payment schemes set to favour generational renewal (payments to both young entrants into farming and early-retiring farmers) and additional support for farmers located in mountain and other geographically handicapped areas. All in all, structural measures had only extremely limited funding and never had the chance of becoming more than just a very modest complement to the market-intervention measures that constituted the CAP's backbone.

The CAP as subsidies (1992 to the present)

Starting in 1992, the EU has gradually deactivated its market-intervention devices. Guaranteed prices, in particular, have been fixed at ever-lower levels, which has brought them ever closer to international market prices. The other devices, such as intervention buying and export subsidies, have eventually become residual. Thirty years after its implementation, one of the strongest instruments of market intervention, dairy quotas, has been discontinued. Over the last quarter century, European farmers have had to manage a transition from EU-intervened markets to ever-freer markets (Ackrill 2000; Reig 2013).

Market intervention was gradually substituted with direct subsidies (Figure 2.1). The reform of the CAP led by the Irish commissioner Ray MacSharry brought about in 1992 the creation of a system of direct payments to farmers. These payments have become the CAP's main instrument and, consequently, the political debate has recurrently revolved around them, especially when it comes to the definition of the subsidy-granting criteria (Ackrill 2000; García Grande 2005; Swinnen 2008, 2015).

The criteria for farmers to receive a subsidy have evolved in three ways over the quarter century that separates us from the MacSharry reform. First, there has

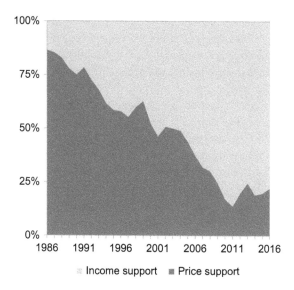

FIGURE 2.1 Composition of public support to farmers in the European Union

Source: OECD (2017).

been a trend towards decoupling payments from production. The payments of the MacSharry reform were not directly linked to production – that is, what the EU would pay to each farmer did not depend on whether the farmer produced more or less. There was, however, an indirect link: subsidies were granted depending on the number of hectares in cultivation and the number of head of livestock on the farm, there being different coefficients for different crops and animals. Therefore, the decisions made by farmers about what to produce and how much to produce had some influence on the amount of the subsidy to be realized (and vice versa).

After the reform led by the Austrian commissioner Franz Fischler in 2003, this link between subsidy and production became almost completely erased. Fischler's subsidies could be granted by the member states according to a variety of possible criteria, but most were unrelated to farmers' production decisions. Some states (France, Italy and Spain among them) opted for the so-called historical criteria: the subsidy realized today was calculated in relation to the subsidy that had been realized a few years earlier, no matter what had happened on the farm since. Others (like Germany) favoured the so-called regional criteria: the subsidy realized by farmers in a given region was calculated in relation to their cultivated area, but by means of coefficients that did not make any distinction between different crops and were therefore identical for all farmers in the region. Actually, there was a range of hybrid options combining historical and regional criteria, but what all the options had in common was that they broke most of the linkage between what farmers chose to do (or not to do) on their farms and what the EU was paying them as a subsidy. Of course, the persistence of some indirect link was still unavoidable: any subsidy, even those that were not formally linked to production, was to lower its recipients' fixed costs (Brassley 1997: 94; Cardwell 2004: 323). But only one direct link survived between production decisions and subsidies: those member states who wanted to were entitled to continue granting a secondary part of their subsidies according to MacSharry criteria, that is, in relation to coefficients that were specific to each crop or animal.

Alongside this trend to decoupling payments from production, the criteria have evolved in two other directions: by creating some differences between large and small farmers, and by treating those farmers who are engaged in environmentally positive practices differently from those who are not. The MacSharry payments treated large and small farmers similarly: the criteria were perfectly proportional to farm size. In 1999 Fischler, however, created the option for member states to modulate their subsidies, so that payments to large farmers would be proportionally less sizeable than payments to smaller ones. In other words, the same hectare of cultivated land would generate a bigger payment right in the hands of a small farmer than to a larger one. With the reform instigated by Fischler again in 2003, this social modulation of subsidies became compulsory for all member states.

A similar sequence of events unfolded in the case of the introduction of environmental criteria. The MacSharry payments did not differentiate between farmers according to the degree of environmental sustainability in their practices. In 1999, Fischler introduced the option for member states to make the subsidy conditional upon the fulfilment of a number of environmental requisites, basically not being engaged in agricultural practices that were clearly harmful to the environment. The following reform in 2003 turned this voluntary option into a compulsory measure for all member states.

The payments scheme that applies today is the one that was passed under the leadership of Romanian commissioner Damian Cioloş in 2013. The current scheme makes more than a few changes in the details of the Fischler scheme, but mostly reinforces the directions alluded to above. There is a basic payment that is calculated from regional coefficients and is delinked from farmers' production decisions, except in those states that choose to apply input-related criteria for a maximum value of 15 per cent of their expenditure. The basic payment is subject to some social modulation: beyond a threshold of 150,000 euros of annual subsidy, a capping of 5 per cent may apply; and only "active farmers" are eligible, which is aimed at excluding large non-agricultural companies that had traditionally been subsidy recipients. In addition to this basic payment, every farmer can apply for a green payment in case they are engaged in what their state defines as environmentally valuable practices. There are other payment regimes, both compulsory for all states (such as payments to young farmers) and voluntary (among them, payments to farmers in areas facing geographical handicaps and a simplified payment regime for very small farmers), but the essentials of the current CAP lie in the basic payment and the green payment.

Alongside these changes in the criteria for granting subsidies, another important transformation has been the emergence of the "second pillar" of CAP (Lowe et al. 2002; Castillo and Ramos 2010). Direct payments to farmers are by far the most important part of the CAP, but they have been joined by policies for the promotion of rural development. This second pillar, created in the 1990s under the leadership of (again) commissioner Fischler, included previously existing measures, especially the structural policies that had been created in the 1970s (pro-competitiveness subsidies, early retirement benefits, payments to young farmers, compensatory allowances for mountain farmers). It also incorporated the "agri-environmental" payments that had been created by MacSharry a few years ago: at a time when the environment did not play any part in the price-based or in the payment-based elements of the first pillar, agri-environmental payments would reward those farmers whose agrarian practices had a very high ecological value.

The second pillar also introduced as a novelty a number of measures set to pro-mote economic and social development in rural areas, which were understood as more than just a site for farming. New funds were made available for the improve-ment of infrastructures in rural areas. There was also support for the diversifica-tion of rural economies that is, the transition from a local economy that was very dependent on agriculture to another one in which industry, construction and ser-vices would be more relevant. Even the LEADER initiative, which had origin-ally been born as a Community Initiative outside the CAP, became a part of the CAP's second pillar. Starting in 1991, the European Commission had been using LEADER as a means to foster public–private partnerships for the promotion of non-agricultural activities in rural areas. It was a novel approach in terms of govern-ance, too: it was up to the so-called local action groups, mainly composed of civil society members, to take the initiative by identifying priority targets and designing multi-year investment plans that would be funded by a combination of European and national/regional sources. In 2007, LEADER was incorporated into the CAP's second pillar, and today it is even possible for national/regional governments to rely on LEADER-type governance when it comes to managing the other instruments belonging to the second pillar (Esparcia et al. 2015).

The second pillar has never reached the funding levels of the first pillar, but it has succeeded at consolidating as a more visible complement of the CAP's backbone than the pre-existing structural policy. Rural development has come to absorb some 15–20 per cent of CAP expenditure (to be compared to hardly 5 per cent for struc-tural measures in the 1970s and 1980s), and member states are allowed to transfer a substantial portion of their first-pillar expenditure (up to 30 per cent) to the second pillar if they wish to strengthen the rural development dimension of the CAP.

To sum up, the CAP of today is very different from the classic CAP that was in force until 1992. Direct subsidies have replaced market intervention as the main instrument for supporting European farmers. Moreover, the CAP's first pillar has been joined by a series of active policies in the areas of agricultural growth, environ-mental sustainability and rural development. Furthermore, in contrast to the relative stability of the classic CAP, over the last quarter century the CAP has been involved in repeated reforms that have resulted in continuous changes in the subsidy-granting criteria. There is an ongoing trend towards subsidies that are less and less linked to production and more and more conditioned to good agri-environmental practices.

In all of this we find a clear break between the CAP of today and the classic CAP. We now review one further element of discontinuity between both paradigms of agricultural policy: the transition from a clearly supranational policy to a reformed CAP in which member states have more room for making their own decisions.

From common to "re-nationalized" policy

The classic CAP, with instruments and parameters that were basically similar all across the EEC, was truly common. The instruments of market intervention, in particular, were applied in a similar way in all member states. Political prices were fixed for the EEC as a whole and, beyond the deviations derived from exchange-rate fluctuations between national currencies, there were not any differences from country to country. The EEC rules for both intervention buying and export subsidies were also similar for all member states.

The CAP was actually not just a policy of farm support, but also a policy aimed at the construction of a single European market. Prior to 1962, each country had its own instruments and parameters of market intervention. For instance, each country had its own trade policy to regulate agricultural relations with the rest of the world. The creation of the CAP and its common tariff implied, however, the dissolution of these national protectionisms into a single, EEC-level protectionism and the abolition of any trade barriers between member states. That is, even though the CAP retained trade protection in relation to third countries (and, as we will see, it actually brought about an increase in the level of that protection), it dismantled the trade barriers that had been separating European neighbours from one another. Member states, then, made a remarkable transfer of sovereignty to EEC institutions. States retained their powers of decision in other areas of agricultural policy – for instance active policies for farm modernization – but lost them in the area that had until then been the hard core of public intervention in agriculture.

Another aspect that made the CAP part of a broader project of European institution-building was its financing. States agreed that the CAP would be funded according to the principle of financial solidarity. There would not be national contributions to the CAP, but direct funding from the EEC budget. Evidently, this reinforced the degree of autonomy of the EEC institutions in charge of designing and implementing agricultural policy.

The contrast to the CAP of today is striking. Today member states have considerable powers of decision over the implementation of farm subsidies. The EU establishes that only "active farmers" can receive payments, but what an active farmer is (or is not) is decided by each member state. The EU establishes that the basic payment, the green payment and the payment to young farmers will be granted everywhere, but four other payment regimes are of voluntary application for member states: the redistributive payment (in order to transfer funding from the first to the second pillar), production-linked support, support to farmers in naturally handicapped areas, and simplified payment for very small farmers. Even within the compulsory payment regimes, there is some margin of discretion for states. This is so, especially in the case of the green payment: the EU establishes that at least 30 per cent of expenditure must be absorbed by the green payment, but it is up to each state to define for itself what valuable environmental practice means, and it is possible to do so in a way that implies a green-payment expenditure in excess of the 30 per cent threshold. The CAP reform process that Irish commissioner Phil Hogan started (and that, at the time of writing, is likely to be completed by Polish commissioner Janusz Wojciechowski) would enter into force in 2021 and is not well defined yet, but one thing seems clear from the initial round of proposals and negotiations: member states will be given even more powers of decision over the definition and implementation of farm-support instruments (European Commission 2018).

States are even more important when it comes to defining and implementing the second pillar, the rural development policy. Today this policy is structured around six objectives: innovation, competitiveness, food-chain organization, ecosystem preservation, transition to low-carbon agriculture, social inclusion and rural development. A wide variety of actions and measures are potentially eligible here, and defining the strategic orientations that will be given priority is basically up to the states (or, in some cases, to their regional governments). The only restriction that states are set by the EU is that environment-related objectives absorb at least 30 per cent of their expenditure in second pillar. Beyond that, the hands of national/regional governments are free.

The "re-nationalization" of agricultural policy is becoming apparent in terms of funding as well. The principle of financial solidarity remains in force for the first pillar, but a principle of co-financing applies to the second pillar. This means that only a proportion of the expenditure on rural development executed in each state is financed by the EU budget: the rest has to be funded by the budget of that particular state. In a way, it has always been like this – the structural policy that was implemented in the 1970s and that constitutes the embryo of today's second pillar was already co-financed. But the consolidation of the second pillar as a more important, better-funded policy has implied that co-financing applies to a larger share of CAP expenditure than had been the case during the CAP's classic era. During the initial round of proposals for the post-2020 CAP, the Commission even posed the possibility of introducing co-financing instruments in the first pillar, so that a proportion of farm subsidies would be paid for by each state, instead of the whole subsidy being paid for by the EU only. It does not seem that this proposal has any chance of making it into the short-run agenda of political negotiations, but it gives a good illustration of the way in which re-nationalization of the CAP may proceed in the future.

As a matter of fact, there seems to be a close connection between re-nationalization and CAP reform. As long as the CAP was a stable policy, it was a common policy, too. Once the CAP took a path of recurrent reform, there has been a trend towards the recognition of all sorts of national details and exceptions. In 1999, the introduction of social and environmental criteria for granting farm subsidies was passed as a voluntary measure for those states that wished to go in that direction and, even though this measure eventually became compulsory for all member states, the latter have retained considerable powers of decision over the key parameters involved. In 2003, the Fischler reform broke most of the link between subsidy and production, but it did so by substituting the compact payment scheme designed by MacSharry by a variety of possible options for member states, ranging from the choice between historical versus regional criteria (or some sort of hybrid between the two) to the choice of retaining (or not) an element of MacSharry-style production-linked support. That was also the time when a special transitory regime was passed in relation to the countries in Central and Eastern Europe that were about to enter the EU. As a result, during the period 2007–2013 farm subsidies in these countries were calculated according to coefficients that were clearly different from (and less remunerative than) those applied in the rest of the Union (Cardwell 2004: 388–392). Finally, the rural development policy has always been given widely different orientations by different national and regional administrations (Lowe et al. 2002; Rosell et al. 2010).

The CAP in the world

Where does the CAP fit within the bigger picture of agricultural policies in the world? Is it a European peculiarity that stands in striking contrast to the experiences in other parts of the world? Or is it a policy that resembles others?

When it comes to having a policy that provides support to farmers, Europe is anything but peculiar. The United States and Japan, for instance, have applied that sort of policy since the 1930s. A more general comparative analysis reveals that the policies of farm support are more common precisely in highly industrialized countries in which farmers are already a minority occupational group (Lindert 1991; Federico 2005; Anderson 2009). The case of the EU and its CAP fits the pattern. In poorer countries, conversely, until the late twentieth century it was policies of an opposite sign that were common: policies that extracted resources from agriculture by setting low agricultural prices, the effect of which was reinforced by the existence of pro-manufacturing, pro-urban biases in industry and trade policies. An indicator that allows us to perceive the historical contrast between pro-agricultural bias in the global North and anti-agricultural bias in the South is the nominal rate of assistance to agriculture. This is a measure of the additional income that farmers gain as a result of favourable policies, put in relation to farmers' income in case those policies had not been implemented. When the rate is negative, it shows the income that unfavourable policies take away from farmers (Figure 2.2).

The peculiarities of the CAP within the bigger picture of agricultural policy in the developed world are not very significant. When the European Commission talks about a distinctively European model of agriculture (Cardwell 2004), or when critics such as Federico (2009: 263) point at the EU as one of the "bad boys" of world agricultural protection, there is some exaggeration in both claims. It is true that the nominal rate of assistance in Figure 2.2 has been traditionally higher in Europe than in the United States, but this indicator does not allow for a firm conclusion. The nominal rate of assistance does not consider those forms of farm support

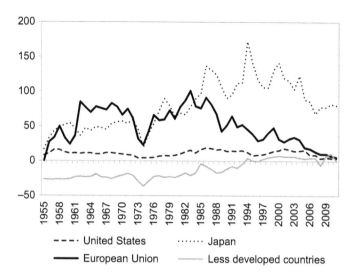

FIGURE 2.2 Nominal rate of assistance to agriculture (%)[a]

Source: Anderson and Nelgen (2013).
[a] Ratio of income transferred to farmers by means of public intervention in agricultural markets to income that farmers would have had in the absence of intervention.

that are decoupled from production, but only those that are based in the public inter-vention of agricultural markets and that would therefore imply a distortion of the ideal of a fully efficient market economy (Anderson 2009: 11–13). This is consistent with the neoclassical tradition from which this indicator originated, but is not very useful for our purposes. The importance of decoupled support has been uneven through time and space, so that excluding it from the calculation distorts the results. For instance, in the case of the European Union, Figure 2.2 suggests that agricultural support has been falling steadily during the last thirty years and has become almost zero today, but this is actually a statistical illusion created by the fact that (as we have seen) the EU has grad-ually substituted its traditional instruments of market intervention (computed in the nominal rate of assistance) with direct payments (not computed).

A more reliable indicator for comparing agricultural support across countries is the "producer subsidy equivalent" calculated by the OECD, which considers both market-intervention measures and direct subsidies. The results in Table 2.1, while retaining the contrast between the global North and the global South, provide a more nuanced view of agricultural support in the North. The contrast between the EU and the United States is less marked here. The EU has actually granted its farmers a level of support very close to the OECD average, somewhere between Japan's huge level and the United States' more moderate but still remarkable level.

To this we must add one further technical detail that affects both the indicator in Figure 2.2 and the indicator in Table 2.1. In both cases, public support to farmers is put in relation to the latter's income. This is a reasonable option, since it favours an intuitive interpretation of the results: for instance, according to the last column

TABLE 2.1 Public support to farmers as a percentage of farm income[a]

	Late 1960s	1986	2000	2016
OECD (total)		37	33	19
European Union	42–47	39	31	21
United States	30	24	23	9
Japan		65	60	48
Developing countries[b]	–8[c]	–3[d]		
Brazil			7	5
China			4	15
Russia			1	16

Sources: Federico (2011: 130–131, 134); OECD (2017).
Notes: [a] Ratio of "producer subsidy equivalent" to gross farm income (%). The "producer subsidy equivalent" is the sum of the support given to farmers through market intervention (additional farm income made possible by the sale of commodities at prices above those that would have resulted from free market forces) and direct subsidies.
[b] Sample of 18 countries; the data are expressed as a percentage of agricultural GDP.
[c] 1960/69.
[d] 1980/83.

in Table 2.1, 21 per cent of the average EU farmer's income comes from the CAP, while the remaining 79 per cent is gained on the market. One problem with these kinds of indicators, though, is that they are very sensitive to exogenous variations in farm income. As a result, the indicators vary through time even if agricultural policies do not. For instance, technical changes, new forms of commercialization and short-run, demand-induced inflationary pressures all may cause an increase in farm income, which would cause a decrease in the relative magnitude of public support. The same policy would have different relative impacts under different exogenous market conditions. On an international scale, productivity differences between farmers may lead to the paradoxical result that two broadly similar agricultural policies have widely different ratios of "producer subsidy equivalent" to farm income.

This problem does not really have a solution: it just forces us to be cautious when making comparisons through time and space and, insofar as it is possible, to complete the analysis with alternative, similarly imperfect indicators. One of these may be the level of agricultural support per person employed in agriculture, which allows us to compare farm support in different periods and countries independently from differences in agricultural productivity. Table 2.2 shows the results for the present and gives an image that is very different from that given by previous indicators. Following this indicator, public support to farmers would be substantially lower in the European Union than in the United States. In some sense, European farmers receive fewer subsidies than their American counterparts. It is their lower level of productivity that makes those subsidies represent a larger share of their income. This is something that researchers have been noting since at least the 1990s (see for instance Buckwell 1997: 159). The conclusion is that it is not evident which of the two policies, the European or the American, lends more support to farmers.

TABLE 2.2 Producer subsidy equivalent (PSE), 2015/18

	European Union	United States
Total PSE (million dollars)	95,636	38,105
PSE as a percentage of farm income	19.3	9.6
PSE per person employed in agriculture (dollars)	9,986	16,943

Sources: OECD (2018); International Labour Organization (www.ilo.org – Ilostat).

TABLE 2.3 Percentage of agricultural support granted via prices

	1986	1996	2006	2016
European Union	87	58	37	22
United States	30	46	15	21
Japan	90	91	88	80

Source: OECD (2017). The remaining support is granted via subsidies.

Anyway, and beyond the necessary relativism with which these support indicators must be interpreted, there is a striking convergence between the EU and the United States when it comes to the instruments chosen to support farmers (Table 2.3). The US policy of farm support had been a policy of market intervention in its origins in the 1930s and even more so during the Second World War, but later on reoriented towards direct subsidies (Gardner 2009: 187–188; González et al. 2016: 68–75). This created a temporary contrast, which was particularly apparent in the 1980s, between a US policy based on income support and a European CAP based on price support. Over the last quarter century, however, the change of paradigm that has taken place in the CAP, in combination with some recoupling of agricultural support and production in the United States since the turn of the millennium (Cardwell 2004: 333, 356; Cunha and Swinbank 2011: 129–130), has almost completely blurred that contrast. In a way, the CAP has "Americanized" or, perhaps more precisely, has "re-Americanized".

In other words: paradoxical as it may seem, precisely at the time when the Commission began to wave the flag of the European model of agriculture in opposition to the US model, the CAP's way of delivering agricultural support came to resemble more the American model than before. Beyond the rhetorical construction of a European agricultural identity, even commissioner Fischler could not help admitting in 2001 (that is, in the midst of the discursive escalade of the European model of agriculture) that "we both wish to pursue domestic support policies, so we share the same policy objective" (cf. Cardwell 2004: 332). Very different was the position held by Canada, Australia, Argentina and a number of developing countries: that agricultural support had to be dismantled, which, in Fischler's view, reflected "a fundamental difference of approach". As a matter of fact, the truly distinctive case is that of Japan, where agricultural support has remained much higher and much more reliant on market intervention than in Europe or the United States.

If anything, the European difference lies in the major transfer of political sovereignty from member states to the Union's supranational institutions. Over the last half century, there has not been any comparable experience of integration of national agricultural policies into a single policy to be designed and funded by supranational institutions. In fact, there has not even been progress as great as could have been expected on the lower step of the ladder – the international coordination of national agricultural policies. From the end of the Second World War and almost up to the fall of the Berlin Wall, there was great progress, led by the GATT, in the liberalization of international industrial markets, but agriculture was excluded from these negotiations. Only during the Uruguay round of the GATT (1986–1993) was agriculture incorporated into international trade negotiations. And, in spite of gaining some initial momentum, the project of liberalizing global agricultural markets has encountered strong opposition at both political and social levels on different geographical scales. The collapse of the agricultural section of the Doha round of the World Trade Organization in the early years of this millennium was the most visible outcome of this resistance (Pritchard 2009).

Under these conditions, the wave of "re-nationalization" that the CAP has been going through since the 1990s should not distract us from the fact that, from a broader perspective, Europe's supranational experience remains unique. It is here, and not actually in the characteristics of the CAP itself, that we find the true peculiarity of the European model of agriculture.

Conclusion

Already more than twenty years ago, historian and economist Paul Brassley (1997: 127) warned that "[in] detail, the Common Agricultural Policy […] is now so complex that there is probably no one person in the whole world who understands completely how every bit of it works". In the time that has passed since, the complexity of the CAP has increased steadily as a result of the incorporation of new instruments and of the "re-nationalization" of a great number of practical details involved in their application. Faced with the task of describing the CAP, this chapter has abandoned any ambition to cover each and every measure that has been (or is) part of this policy. A stylized description in terms of "policy paradigms" has been proposed instead.

More specifically, two distinct paradigms have been identified in the history of the CAP. The first is the original CAP, which, roughly speaking, was in force between 1962 and 1992. This was a policy based on the intervention of agricultural markets: agricultural prices were set at artificially high levels, and the resulting overproduction was dealt with by means of public purchases of surplus production, export subsidies and (to a lesser extent) quantitative restrictions to production.

These mechanisms of market intervention were for the most part designed and applied on a supranational scale. European institutions positioned this early CAP as a social-justice policy aimed at ensuring that farmers reached a living standard comparable to that of the rest of the citizens. Both in its instruments and in its discourse, the original CAP actually belonged to the agricultural policy paradigm that prevailed in the member states prior to the creation of the European Economic Community (Knudsen 2009: 266).

The change of paradigm was started by the MacSharry reform of 1992 and consolidated by the Fischler reform of 2003. Other, minor reforms, have introduced additional adjustments and modifications over the last quarter century. The key to paradigm change was the substitution of a system of price support via market intervention with a system of income support via direct payments to farmers. The criteria for the granting of said payments have also gone through repeated transformations, especially in the direction of making agricultural support less dependent on production and more on environmental and territorial values. These changes in the CAP have taken place in parallel to a renovation in the European Union's discourse, in which the traditional dimension of social justice has been joined by a vindication of agricultural multifunctionality and an allegedly distinctive European model of agriculture.

That this European model of agriculture is truly distinctive is a different matter, though. In agriculture, as in other areas, the image of coordinated capitalism as something exceptional (and liberal capitalism as the general case) does not hold. As a matter of fact, the original CAP belonged to an agricultural policy paradigm that was in large measure present in other parts of the developed world such as the United States and Japan. The persistence of these policies of agricultural support in more recent times, combined with the implementation of policies of agricultural support in China and other parts of the developing world, has made agrarian coordinated capitalism anything but a European hallmark. The image of a so-called European model of agriculture being defined in contrast to the US model does not hold either. Actually, the CAP has tended to "Americanize" as successive reforms have substituted market-intervention measures with direct subsidies as the main instrument of farm support. As in the broader debate on Europe's economic and social model, it is likely that both the supporters and the critics of the model have taken for granted Europe's alleged difference and have omitted the existence of lines of convergence in relation to the United States.

References

Ackrill, R. 2000. *The Common Agricultural Policy*. Sheffield: Sheffield Academic Press.

Anderson, K. 2009. "Five decades of distortions to agricultural incentives". In *Distortions to agricultural incentives: A global perspective, 1955–2007*, ed. K. Anderson, 3–64. Washington, DC: World Bank and Palgrave Macmillan.

Anderson, K. and Nelgen, S. 2013. "Updated national and global estimates of distortions to agricultural incentives, 1955 to 2011", www.worldbank.org/agdistortions.

Brassley, P. 1997. *Agricultural economics and the CAP: An introduction*. Oxford: Blackwell.

Buckwell, A. 1997. "Some microeconomic analysis of CAP market regimes". In *The Common Agricultural Policy*, eds. C. Ritson and D. R. Harvey (eds.), 139–162. Wallingford: CAB International.

Cardwell, M. 2004. *The European model of agriculture*. Oxford: Oxford University Press.

Castillo, J. S. and Ramos, E. 2010. "El nuevo desarrollo rural y el futuro de la política rural en la Unión Europea". In *"Chequeo médico" de la PAC y perspectivas de la Política Agraria Común tras 2013*, coords. J. M. García Álvarez-Coque and J. A. Gómez Limón, 177–212. Madrid: Eumedia and Ministerio de Medio Ambiente y Medio Rural y Marino.

Cunha, A. and Swinbank, A. 2011. *An inside view of the CAP reform process: Explaining the MacSharry, Agenda 2000, and Fischler reforms*. Oxford: Oxford University Press.

Esparcia, J., Escribano, J., and Serrano, J. J. 2015. "From development to power relations and territorial governance: increasing the leadership role of LEADER Local Action Groups in Spain". *Journal of Rural Studies* 42: 29–42.

European Commission. 2012. *The Common Agricultural Policy: A story to be continued*. Luxembourg: Office for Official Publications of the European Communities.

European Commission. 2018. "EU budget: The Common Agricultural Policy beyond 2020", MEMO 18/3974.

Federico, G. 2005. *Feeding the world: An economic history of world agriculture, 1800–2000*. Princeton: Princeton University Press.

Federico, G. 2009. "Was the CAP the worst agricultural policy of the 20th century?". In *Fertile ground for Europe? The history of European integration and the Common Agricultural Policy since 1945*, ed. K. K. Patel, 257–271. Baden-Baden: Nomos.

Federico, G. 2011. *Breve historia económica de la agricultura*. Zaragoza: Prensas Universitarias de Zaragoza and Institución Fernando el Católico.

Freeman, C. and Louçã, F. 2001. *As time goes by: From the industrial revolutions to the information revolution*. Oxford: Oxford University Press.

García Delgado, J. L. and García Grande, M. J. 2005. "Nacimiento y desarrollo de una idea: de la conferencia de Stressa en 1958 a la reforma MacSharry en 1992". In *Política agraria común: balance y perspectivas*, coords. J. L. García Delgado and M. J. García Grande, 17–43. Barcelona: La Caixa.

García Grande, M. J. 2005. "El último decenio: aplicación y consecuencias de las reformas de la PAC". In *Política agraria común: balance y perspectivas*, coords. J. L. García Delgado and M. J. García Grande, 44–69. Barcelona: La Caixa.

Gardner, B. 1996. *European agriculture: Policies, production and trade*. London: Routledge.

Gardner, B. L. 2009. "United States and Canada". In *Distortions to agricultural incentives: A global perspective, 1955–2007*, ed. K. Anderson, 177–220. Washington, DC: World Bank and Palgrave Macmillan.

González, Á. L., Pinilla, V., and Serrano, R. 2016. "International agricultural markets after the war, 1945–1960". In *Agriculture in capitalist Europe, 1945–1960: from food shortages to food surpluses*, eds. C. Martiin, J. Pan-Montojo and P. Brassley, 64–84. Farnham: Ashgate.

Hall, P. A. 1993. "Policy paradigms, social learning and the State. The case of economic policy-making in Britain". *Comparative Politics* 25 (3): 275–296.

Kay, A. 2006. *The dynamics of public policy: Theory and evidence*. Cheltenham: Edward Elgar.

Knudsen, A.-C. L. 2009. *Farmers on welfare: The making of Europe's Common Agricultural Policy*. Ithaca, NY: Cornell University Press.

Lindert, P. H. 1991. "Historical patterns of agricultural policy". In *Agriculture and the state: Growth, employment, and poverty in developing countries*, ed. C. P. Timmer, 29–83. Ithaca, NY: Cornell University Press.

Lovec, M. 2016. *The European Union's Common Agricultural Policy reforms*. London: Palgrave Macmillan.

Lowe, P., Buller, H. and Ward, N. 2002. "Setting the next agenda? British and French approaches to the second pillar of the Common Agricultural Policy". *Journal of Rural Studies* 18 (1): 1–17.

OECD. 2017. *Agricultural support estimates – 2017 edition*, https://stats.oecd.org.

OECD. 2018. *Agricultural policy monitoring and evaluation 2018*. Paris: OECD.

Pritchard, B. 2009. "The long hangover from the second food regime: A world-historical interpretation of the collapse of the WTO Doha Round". *Agriculture and Human Values* 26 (4): 297–307.

Reig, E. 2013. "La Política Agraria Común". In *Economía de la Unión Europea*, dirs. J. M. Jordán and C. Tamarit, 375–400. Madrid: Civitas and Thomson Reuters.

Rosell, J., Viladomiu, L. and Correa, M. 2010. "Mejora del medio ambiente y nivel de desarrollo: las opciones de los Programas de Desarrollo Rural (2007–2013) de la Unión Europea". *Revista Española de Estudios Agrosociales y Pesqueros* 226: 13–37.

Swinnen, J. F. M. 2008. "The political economy of the Fischler reforms of the EU's Common Agricultural Policy: the perfect storm?". In *The perfect storm: The political economy of the Fischler reforms of the Common Agricultural Policy*, ed. J. F. M. Swinnen, 135–166. Brussels: Centre for European Policy Studies.

Swinnen, J. F. M. 2015. "An imperfect storm in the political economy of the Common Agricultural Policy". In *The perfect storm: The political economy of the Fischler reforms of the Common Agricultural Policy*, ed. J. F. M. Swinnen, 443–484. Brussels: Centre for European Policy Studies.

Tracy, M. 1989. *Government and agriculture in Western Europe, 1880–1988*. New York: New York University Press.

3

THE MONSTER MYTH

Historian Alan Milward (2000: 317) has called the CAP a "clumsy prehistoric mastodon". It is a striking expression, but its mood is far from unique in the field of CAP studies. Many critics of the CAP, ranging from pro-market economists to anti-globalization activists, have argued that its cost is disproportionate. Through artificially high food prices, consumers have been forced to pay for the public support given to farmers. As time has gone by, Europeans have also been increasingly forced to pay for the CAP by means of their taxes. If this were not enough, the populations living in the rest of the world, in poor countries in particular, have also suffered from the effects of the EU's agricultural policy. What a disaster! Or, remembering the third of Carlo Maria Cipolla's (1991) laws of human stupidity, that is: that stupid people cause losses to other people without getting any benefit for themselves (or even getting their own losses); what a stupidity!

But, are these arguments correct? This chapter argues that the costs of the CAP are smaller and less serious than it may seem. The organization of the chapter is as follows. The first section examines the costs borne by consumers, while the second section examines the costs borne by taxpayers. The third section analyses the impact of the CAP upon the global South and world poverty. The conclusions recapitulate in order to argue that the costs and impacts of the CAP have been more moderate than is commonly suggested.

A heavy burden on consumers?

Critics are right that for a long time the CAP has forced European consumers to pay for their food more than should have been necessary. This is especially evident in the case of the classic CAP. Since it was based mostly on setting agricultural prices above those that would have been arrived at in a free-market situation, most of the support given to farmers by the classic CAP was paid for by the consumers.

In a way, it is as if the CAP had been financed by means of a tax on food consumption. To make things worse, it is almost certain that this tax burden was heavier for low-income consumers, who devoted a larger share of their expenditure to buying basic necessities such as food (Gardner 1996: 58–59; Judt 2005: 307).

But, how heavy was this load? Figure 3.1 gives us a first approximation by showing the difference between agricultural prices in the European market, inflated (so to speak) by the CAP, and agricultural prices in the international market. Prior to the MacSharry reform, agricultural prices were indeed substantially higher in Europe – around 60 per cent higher. We can compare this figure to a gap of around 40–50 per cent prior to the implementation of the CAP (Milward 2000: 260). The conclusion is that it is quite likely that the CAP aggravated a historical trend that had roots in previous periods. An agricultural policy less oriented towards market intervention would have allowed European prices to align with those prevailing in the world market, as has actually happened during the period of reforms that has transformed the CAP in a system of direct subsidies.

The problem is that this first approximation is too crude and overestimates the real cost borne by consumers. This is so because of both technical issues related to our indicator and a more substantial issue related to the context of consumption and nutrition during this period.

The technical issue is this: our indicator exaggerates the impact of agricultural policies on the price of food. To begin with, the "world market price" is not really independent from the agricultural policy decisions made by the largest countries (or groups of countries). During the era of the classic CAP, the EEC dumped increasing volumes of agricultural produce into the world market at prices that

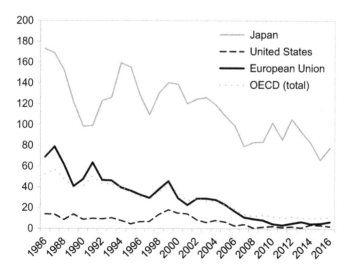

FIGURE 3.1 Difference between domestic market prices and world market prices as a consequence of agricultural policies (%)

Source: OECD (2017).

were below those prevailing in the European market. Therefore, the agricultural prices that were actually observable in the world market were lower than prices that would have been arrived at in a situation of no intervention on the part of the EEC. Some estimates suggest that this effect explains around one fourth of the price gap that can be observed at the beginning of Figure 3.1's timeline (Gardner 1996: 58).

But, what about the remaining three fourths? Do they not clearly prove that the European consumer was forced to carry a heavy load? Not so clearly, indeed. What the European consumer would buy was not agricultural commodities, but food products; that is, products that had undergone some industrial processing or, at the very least, would have circulated through a chain of commercial inter-mediaries beyond the farm gate. In other words, the price of the food products bought by consumers depended on the farm gate price of raw materials, but also (and increasingly more so) on the costs and profits applied by the other links in the food chain (Malassis 1997: 194–195; Ackrill 2000: 206). As a consequence, the fact that agricultural products were (say) 45 per cent more expensive than they would have been without intervention policies does not mean that food products could have been 45 per cent cheaper. If the cost of raw agricultural products amounted to (say) half of the food price paid by the consumer, then eliminating the agricul-tural price gap of 45 per cent would have reduced food prices by 22.5 per cent only. It is striking to observe that during the 1990s, as European agricultural prices were beginning to converge to world agricultural prices, food prices evolved in a much more rigid way (Andreosso-O'Calaghan 2003: 241–242). During those years highly processed foodstuffs were becoming more and more important in the diet of Europeans (Malassis 1997), which implied that the price of raw agricultural products was becoming less and less important in the formation of consumer food prices.

The conclusion from these technical details is that the CAP, even in its classic version, has not been as damaging to consumers as a hurried reading of Figure 3.1 might suggest. Some economists have estimated that, after these technical details have been polished, the extra price that the CAP was forcing European consumers to pay was around 15 per cent (Ritson 1997: 247). Still, for most economists this is bad enough. However, the gravity of this undercover tax must be assessed instead of simply being taken for granted (as is usually the case in the world of "Econ 101"). We must evaluate the gravity of consumer losses in the context of the changes that were taking place in consumption and nutrition in Europe during the decades after the Second World War.

By the time the CAP was implemented, the consumption patterns of Europeans were moving further and further away from food and basic needs. The 1960s, in particular, were crucial for the making of a mass consumer society in which more and more households would channel increasing shares of their expenditure towards the purchase of cars, household appliances and real estate property (Table 3.1). In more recent times we have been witness to successive new cycles of this consumer society, but one thing is clear: food absorbs an ever-decreasing share of consumer expenditure. As a result, the consumer losses inflicted by the CAP are not at all as serious as they would have been in societies such as those of the nineteenth

TABLE 3.1 Share of private consumer expenditure absorbed by food in the EU's largest member states (%)

	France	Germany	Italy	Poland	Spain	United Kingdom
1965/8	29	34	38			25
1988	17	15	24		26	14
2010	16	12	19	23	14	13

Sources: Collantes (2017: 48); Eurostat (ec.europa.eu/eurostat, *Population and social conditions*, "Structure of mean consumption expenditure").

century, when most households were devoting the majority of their income to purchasing food. By the time the CAP was implemented, European consumers were on another level. Of course, this argument is more valid for high-income consumers than for low-income consumers, who spent a higher share of their income on food. But even among lower-income households there was an extraordinary transformation of consumption patterns that involved a substantial reduction of food's share in household expenditure.

Furthermore, we must take into account that there has been a long-term decrease in food prices during the time the CAP has been in force (Malassis 1997). In other words, even though the CAP has made food more expensive, it has done so at a time in history when other factors were making food become much cheaper. These factors include, among others, technological innovation in agriculture, the rise of food processing, and the "retailing revolution" led by a few major supermarket chains. These developments in the food chain have outweighed by far the effect of the CAP on the price of food. By the time the CAP started, the European food system was not that of the nineteenth century anymore. Rather than being exposed to a chronic risk of scarcity and inflation, the food system was actually on its way to excess capacity. This has implied that the burden placed on consumers was much less serious than is often assumed.

Finally, we must realize that, already during the era of the classic CAP the diet of Europeans had ceased to be that of the nineteenth century: poor, insufficient, close to malnutrition. By the 1960s, Europeans were already embarked on what would turn out to be their transition towards an excess-prone diet, with calorie intakes well above those recommended by nutritionists and a dangerously high level of consumption of saturated fats and sugar. This diet has been at the root of new public-health concerns, including obesity and an increase in the prevalence of degenerative diseases (Popkin 1993; Pollan 2008; Pujol and Cussó 2014). Moreover, it is likely that consumers were also embarked on a broader consumerist drive that, in the case of food, involved the substitution of relatively simple products by more sophisticated varieties that could signal status and express self-identity more effectively. This is, however, a path that in recent analysis of welfare in high-consumption societies has been repeatedly identified as problematic (Schwartz 2004; Skidelsky and Skidelsky 2012; Etzioni 2016).

In this context, implementing an undercover tax on food consumption, as the classic CAP did, may have been good (rather than bad) for consumers' actual welfare. This argument on an aggregate level holds as well if we consider the asymmetries with which different groups of agricultural products were treated by the CAP (Ritson 1997: 257–262). Some of the products for which the EEC had the largest price gaps in relation to the world market, such as meat and dairy, were the products with the highest content of saturated fats. Conversely, more healthy foods, such as fruits and vegetables, could be bought at prices that were broadly similar to those in the world market. In other words, the CAP's implicit tax on food consumption happened to be higher for those products that were emerging as a major threat to the health of Europeans, especially when it came to excess intakes of saturated fats and their plausible connection to degenerative diseases. The designers of the CAP did not of course intend to create anything similar to the kind of targeted food taxes that are becoming common today in order to deal with public health concerns, but in retrospect it can be argued that they did alter consumers' incentives precisely in that direction.

The conclusion is that the CAP did not harm the possibilities of European consumers as much as is often suggested and that the actual harm was not as serious as is commonly assumed. Moreover, other dimensions of consumer welfare beyond purchasing power – including the variety of food options made available to consumers – have led some researchers to see the CAP in a more positive light (Ritson 1997). Anyway, the agricultural price gap between the EU and the world market started to narrow in the post-1992 era of reforms, as we have seen. As a matter of fact, only Japan, where price supports remained the backbone of agricultural policy, went on extracting resources from its consumers in a noticeable way. In Europe, the gradual deactivation of market intervention mechanisms made agricultural prices become closer and closer to those prevailing in the world market. Citizens ceased to pay for the CAP as consumers and came to do so almost exclusively as taxpayers.

A heavy burden on taxpayers?

There is no doubt that taxpayers have paid for the CAP and continue to do so. This is evident in the reformed, post-1992 CAP, as direct subsidies financed from the EU budget have become the main instrument of farm support. But also the classic CAP, in spite of being financed mostly by consumers, absorbed resources from the Community budget: the expenditure made by the EEC on purchasing surplus production for farmers and on subsidizing exports. To this we must add the considerable management costs involved in market intervention, especially for the storage of surplus production and the proper functioning of bureaucratic procedures.

Critics of the CAP commonly use two proofs in order to document what they see as a disproportionate budgetary cost. The first is cost in absolute terms. As Swinnen (2018: 110) puts it, "Since [the 1960s] Europe has continued to spend tens of billions of euros every year – the EU alone more than fifty billion – on its farmers". Today, indeed, the CAP costs Europeans more than 55 billion euros. The second is the CAP's share in the EU budget. In Judt's (2005: 307) words, "by 1970 [...] agriculture was costing 70 percent of the budget, a bizarre situation for some of the world's most industrialized states". Today, agriculture's share in the EU budget is lower, but remains above 40 per cent.

Neither of these two proofs, however, is as forceful as it may seem. References to the CAP's absolute cost are meant to have an impact, but much of this impact is based on having the reader compare CAP's numbers with the absolute numbers that will come to their mind most quickly: those of their own household economy. Of course, the CAP then looks like a "gigantic redistribution machine" (the expression, taken from a different context, comes from Patel, 2009: 160), as nearly any other public policy with some relevance would. This cognitive distortion is aggravated by the frequent use of nominal values when measuring over time the evolution of the CAP budget, which is misleading because it prevents extracting inflation from the time series.

The use of the CAP's share in the EU budget induces a cognitive distortion of the same kind. The EU is generally perceived as an important institution, from which it would follow that absorbing as much as 70 per cent (or even 40 per cent) of that institution's budget is a lot. However, the EU budget has always been meagre, and most public expenditure made in the EU countries is financed by the national budgets of its various member states. A policy that absorbs a small share of these national budgets may easily imply a heavier burden on taxpayers than a policy that absorbs 80 per cent of the EU's small budget.

The figure that we really need is the CAP's cost per person in constant values. This is not as simple as it seems because the Commission usually presents its data in current values or, at the most, applies an ad hoc deflator of 2 per cent per year. Moreover, even though the Commission informs about the number of countries that composed the EU at each moment (which surely helps us to have a more nuanced picture of the evolution of CAP expenditure over time), it does not divide expenditure over the number of inhabitants who were living in the Union at each moment. Figure 3.2 provides for the first time a series that faces these difficulties. First, it uses a more realistic deflator. The results obtained with this deflator fit well with one of the very few estimates of CAP expenditure in constant values produced by the Commission: an estimate of growth by a factor of 2.3 during the period 1975–1991 (Cunha and Swinbank 2011: 8), which is barely 0.2 points below our estimate. Second, the data in Figure 3.2 control for changes in the size of the EU's population after each round of enlargement leading to the incorporation of new member states.

The results do not lend support to the alarmist image of huge sums of money flowing from taxpayers to farmers. In the last fifty years, the CAP has cost the taxpayer between 80 and 200 euros per year (Table 3.2). Today we are considerably closer to the first of these figures than to the second one. It is true that the CAP has absorbed a large share of the EU budget, but even so it has always been an almost insignificant fraction of total public spending in Europe (Table 3.3).

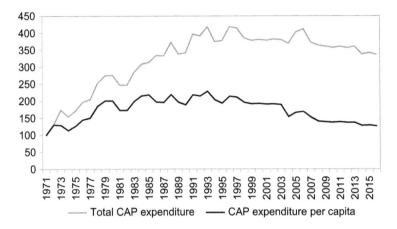

FIGURE 3.2 CAP expenditure in constant values, 1971 = 100

Sources: nominal expenditure: European Commission (2009: 77-81) and Eurostat (ec.europa.eu/ eurostat, *Budget,* "EU expenditure and revenue 2014-2020"); deflator: World Bank (data.worldbank.org, "Inflation – GDP deflator"); population: Eurostat (ec.europa.e/eurostat, *Economy and finance,* "National accounts"), *Maddison project database* (www.ggdc.net/maddison), Statistiches Bundesamt (www.destatis. de, Population).

TABLE 3.2 CAP's cost in relative terms

	1971	*1980*	*1990*	*2000*	*2008*	*2016*
CAP expenditure per person (constant euros of 2016)	87.9	176.5	166.2	169.4	123.0	110.6
Share of CAP in… (%)						
EU budget	82.3	73.2	62.3	53.5	46.2	41.4
Total public expenditure[a]	1.0	1.2	1.2	1.2	0.9	0.8
Gross Domestic Product	0.3	0.6	0.6	0.5	0.4	0.4

Sources: Cost per person: see Figure 3.2; share of CAP expenditure: European Commission (2009: 77–81) and Eurostat (ec.europa.eu/eurostat, *Budget,* "EU expenditure and revenue 2014–2020"; and *Economy and finance,* "Government revenue, expenditure and main aggregates").
Note: [a] Expenditure by all levels of the public sector (European, national, regional and local) in the territory of the European Union.

In fact, the CAP's cost per person only grew quickly during the 1970s. At that time, the incentive structure embedded in the CAP was clearly perverse: there were incentives for farmers to produce as much as possible, regardless of whether or not there was a demand for that production. The higher the production level, the higher the support received by the farmer. The classic CAP disconnected European farmers from the signal that a free market would have sent them to lower their production level: declining prices. For farmers, producing surpluses was not a problem at all. On top of this incentive structure, the fact that the EEC revised its intervention prices in an openly generous way for most of the 1970s (Tracy 1989: Chapter 14) could not lead but to an escalation in CAP expenditure.

TABLE 3.3 Expenditure made by all levels of the public sector in the territory of the
European Union, broken down by type of expenditure (% GDP)

	1995	2005	2016
Social protection	18.8	17.7	19.1
Health	5.9	6.5	7.1
General public services	8.8	6.5	6.0
Education	4.9	5.0	4.7
Economic issues	6.5	4.1	4.0
of which: CAP	0.6	0.5	0.4
Public order, security and defense	3.4	3.3	3.0
Other[a]	2.2	2.4	2.0
Total	51.1	46.0	46.3

Sources: CAP: Table 3.2; rest of data: Eurostat (ec.europa.eu/eurostat, *Economy and finance*, "General
government expenditure by function (COFOG)").
Note: [a] Environmental protection, residential and community amenities, and leisure, culture and religion.

That this escalation continued throughout the following decade, as often can be
read in histories of the CAP, is a half-truth. It is true that, in absolute terms, it did,
as the EEC resisted vigorously applying the only instrument that could stabilize
the classic system of farm support: quantitative restrictions to production. Except
in the dairy sector, quantitative restrictions were introduced at a late date and in
soft versions, which moderated but did not eliminate perverse incentives. The con-
tinuing climb in expenditure in absolute terms led the EEC to an uneasy internal
debate about its budget and the insufficiency of its financing instruments. This
would eventually result in the creation of a new instrument based on each country's
GDP level. Yet, we should not lose sight of the fact that the introduction of some
quantitative restrictions, combined with a price policy that was more austere than
in the previous decades (Tracy 1989: Chapter 14), made possible a containment of
CAP's cost per person. It must be noted that this happened at a time when three
Mediterranean countries were joining the EEC and all three (including one as large
as Spain) would be net receivers of CAP funds because of their economic back-
wardness and their relatively high share of agricultural employment.

The stabilization of the budget cost per capita was the prelude to a clear decrease
in the former from the early 1990s onwards. The main reason was that successive
reforms of the CAP, in particular the MacSharry reform in 1992 and the Fischler
reform in 2003, tended to decouple farm support from farm production. This
eliminated most of the incentives to overproduce. Under MacSharry decoupling
was partial: the new subsidies depended on the number of hectares under cultivation and the number of livestock units in the farm, all of which were computed by
means of product-specific coefficients. Therefore, farmers' decisions about what to
produce were still subject to the influence of MacSharry's coefficients. However,
these product-specific coefficients were combined with a regional productivity
coefficient, which at least diminished the incentives for farmers to maximize the

output they would get from their land and livestock inputs. Furthermore, we should not forget that the MacSharry reform started to deactivate the market intervention system. Substantial cuts in intervention prices, in particular, reduced the incentives to overproduce even more. They also narrowed the gap between the agricultural prices faced by European food industries and those prevailing on the world market, allowing for a reduction of the EU's expenditure on export subsidies.

Under Fischler, the introduction of historical and regional criteria, which by their very nature were not product-specific, implied a stronger decoupling between farm support and farm production. What under the classic CAP was an open-ended system of support with potentially dangerous consequences for the EEC budget became a closed system, the budgetary demands of which could be forecast with remarkable accuracy in the short run. This was joined by the controversial transitory regime that was applied to the new member states from Central and Eastern Europe. These were countries that, for the same reasons as the Mediterranean accession countries in the 1980s, were destined to become net receivers of CAP funds. The Eastern enlargement would actually lead to an increase in the EU's agricultural area and labour force by 50 and 200 per cent, respectively (Swinnen 2018: 118). The application of subsidy coefficients that were markedly less generous than those applied in the rest of the EU allowed for a containment of agricultural expenditure in absolute terms and, even more importantly for our analysis, a clear trend towards its decrease in per capita terms.

The CAP has never been the "gigantic machine" oriented towards resource extraction and redistribution that its critics allude to. As time goes by, it actually moves further and further away from that. If only all of our burdens as taxpayers were as light as this one!

A brake on the development of the global South?

The critics are right that poor countries would have fared better under a European agricultural policy that had not dumped surpluses into their markets and had kept the European market fully open to foreign imports. Around 1960, prior to the CAP, Europe was a net importer of food (Aparicio et al. 2009: 62–63). Barely two decades after that, Europe had become one of the major world exporters of key agricultural commodities such as cereals, meat and milk (Ackrill 2000: 74). The way in which the CAP favoured this shift in Europe's trade position is clear. On the one hand, the CAP implied an increase in the level of protection that trade policy was granting European farmers in relation to their non-European counterparts. Given that, at the same time, the CAP was destroying most of the trade barriers that separated Europe's national farming communities from one another, some of the trade that had been taking place between EEC countries and non-EEC countries became trade within the EEC area. According to some researchers, Europe became a commercial fortress – its walls prevented non-EEC farmers from participating in the European market. By supporting its own producers of (for instance) bananas and sugar, the EEC and later the EU would put a brake on the growth impulses of those southern countries that had traditionally specialized on those commodities (Lingard and Hubbard 1997).

On the other hand, the CAP protected not only farmers. As a means of compensating them for the extra cost implied by agricultural protectionism, the CAP also subsidized those industries and traders that were involved in export activities. These subsidies allowed European exporters to set prices outside the EU that were below those that prevailed inside the EU for identical products. Consequently, European exports into the markets of the global South became higher than they would have been had subsidies not existed (González-Esteban 2017, 2018).

In the short run, Europe's subsidized exports could play a positive role for consumers in the importing countries of the South. This is particularly clear for poor countries that during this period became dependent on food imports and/or went through severe humanitarian crises (Lingard and Hubbard 1997). In the longer run, however, artificially cheap imports from the EU involved unfair competition. In countries such as Kenya and Cameroon, for instance, the domestic production of flour and milk (respectively) could have been higher if domestic farmers and industries had not had to face the competition of CAP-subsidized European multinationals (Fritz 2012: 57–61). Additionally, this would have probably made it easier for these countries to develop the business- and labour-related capabilities that were necessary in order to form stronger agri-food districts as the basis for successive new rounds of economic growth in the longer term. The alternative path, followed in much of Africa, was to become dependent on foreign supplies of food, but this had the problem of making consumers vulnerable to unfavourable fluctuations in world markets – something that they could not expect their governments to have an influence on. The food price spike that took place in 2007–2008 was a good illustration of how a succession of situations that are efficient from a static point of view does not guarantee that there will be a positive trajectory from a dynamic point of view (see a Central American case study in Botella 2012).

It is true that the EU has gradually phased out trade barriers and export subsidies (Table 3.4), but some researchers suggest (and quite rightly so) that both elements have come to be replaced by the direct subsidies given to farmers (Fritz 2012: 40; McMichael 2013; Koning 2017: Chapter 7). The EU subsidizes farmers but, since these sell their produce to a small number of processors involved in monopolistic competition against one another, much of the farm subsidy ends up being absorbed by processors through lower-than-equilibrium agricultural prices.

TABLE 3.4 Share of CAP expenditure devoted to export subsidies (%)

1980	1990	2000	2010
50	29	13	1

Source: European Commission (ec.europa.eu, *Agriculture*, "CAP expenditure and CAP reform path"; *Budget*).

The prices that processors pay for their agricultural raw materials are lower than those that would have been formed in the absence of farm subsidies. This makes it possible for processors, in spite of having lost most of their rights to direct export subsidies, to go on selling at artificially low prices in non-EU markets. In turn, farm subsidies allow EU farmers to retain a level of public support that is not available to their non-EU counterparts, which in a way protects them from the latter.

None of this, however, was (or is) as crucial and devastating for the global South as is commonly assumed by the intellectual front that, on this matter, is made up of neoclassical economists, Marxist sociologists and anti-globalization activists. A more nuanced view is needed. To begin with, and contrary to Gardner (1996: 83) or McMichael (2013), the transformation of the pattern of the world agri-food trade was not at all only a consequence of the CAP. The rise of the EU as an agriculture-exporting power resulted from a more general redefinition of comparative advantage on a global scale. Prior to the Second World War, when the agri-food trade was dominated by simple, relatively unprocessed products, several regions in the non-European world emerged as major producers of commodities that were considered exotic in Europe (for instance, sugar, coffee and bananas). Among other factors, abundant land and suitable climate conditions contributed to this. Conversely, after the Second World War changes in consumer demand have led highly processed foods to become the most dynamic segment in world agri-food trade. This has improved substantially the North's competitive position. On the supply side, the North has the business- and labour-related capabilities that are needed in order to sustain a sophisticated food industry, producing a wide variety of highly processed foods. On the demand side, the North has a strong domestic market, premised upon the widespread participation of affluent middle classes in mass consumer society. On the basis of this strong domestic market, food industries may reach a scale that allows them to reduce their unit costs of production which, in turn, gives them more room to reduce consumer prices both at home and on new export markets (Bairoch 1993: 152–157; Pinilla and Serrano 2009; Aparicio et al. 2018; Pinilla 2018).

To sum up, the EU's position within the international division of agri-food labour is less "politically constructed" (to borrow McMichael's expression; 2013: 17) than it might seem. This forces us to reconsider who are the truly harmed by the EU's policy bias against imports and for exports. Both the external protection given to farmers and the subsidies given to processors have damaged the interests of farmers and processors in other parts of the global North, mostly. There is much exaggeration in the image of large numbers of farmers in the South being fatally hit by the CAP. Many poor countries are located in tropical and subtropical regions where agricultural production is oriented towards commodities that are different from those produced in Europe. Except in the case of a few specific products, such as sugar and bananas, that is not the external competition from which the CAP protects a majority of European farmers specialized on cereals, meat or dairy. The great beneficiaries of a forceful liberalization of Europe's agriculture would not be the poor farmers of the South, but the thriving farmers of the United States and other Western countries (Andreosso-O'Calaghan 2003: 239).

To this we must add the fact that an essential part of the agri-food problems of the South has endogenous causes, rather than resulting from the North's agricultural policies. The making of a strong agri-food chain requires the development of business- and labour-related capabilities, which unfortunately has happened only moderately in many countries of Asia, Latin America and especially Africa. In this respect, the problems of the agri-food sector are not different from those of the other sectors in these economies.

Additionally, the South's agri-food sector has suffered from two problems of its own. First, the agrarian systems of the South have had to face a population boom that, especially during the second half of the twentieth century, went well beyond what the North had experienced in a comparable stage of its development (Cipolla 1974: Chapters 4 and 5; Bairoch 1993: Chapter 12). Very often, the combination of new health technologies and old reproductive habits overflew the production possibilities of local agri-ecosystems. In spite of intense rural-urban migrations, the rural population of the South grew very rapidly (Collantes and Pinilla 2011: 21–25). In many cases, the results of domestic farming fell short of securing food availability for this rapidly growing population (Bairoch 1997, III: 788–845).

Moreover, and second, public policies that were crucial in the North's historical experience for the development of capabilities (Chang 2009) have been weak in the South. Many of these policies have actually contributed to blocking, rather than fostering, progress in the agri-food sector. As a matter of fact, it is these policies, rather than the ones implemented in the North, that are currently prominent in historians' explanations of arrested agricultural development in the South (see, for instance, most of the contributions in the exhaustive compilation by Pinilla and Willebald 2018).

Especially during the period in which the CAP was more protectionist (that is, prior to 1992), most countries in what by then was called the Third World implemented economic policies that were focused on promoting industrialization and paid little attention to agriculture. Similar to the EEC, the countries from the South fixed agricultural prices at levels that were different from those that would have prevailed in a free market situation. However, and contrary to the EEC, they chose price levels that were artificially low. This anti-agrarian bias, intended to transfer resources towards the urban sectors and thus (allegedly) accelerate national development, was particularly marked in Asia, but was present in Latin America and Africa as well (Andersson and Rohne Till 2018: 51; Ash et al. 2018; Booth 2018; Gunnarsson 2018).

The anti-agrarian bias of economic policy was reinforced by fiscal, trade and exchange-rate policies that drained an even greater amount of resources away from agriculture (Table 3.5). In countries with an agri-exporting tradition, for instance in much of Latin America, it was not uncommon for the anti-agrarian bias to be stronger for those products that were more oriented towards exports (Martín-Retortillo et al. 2018: 347–351). Political elites were generally pessimistic about agri-exporting as a driver of economic development. The shift of European and US trade policies towards protectionism during the interwar period (between the two

TABLE 3.5 Income transfers to farmers as a result of public policies in a sample of developing countries (% agricultural GDP)[a]

	1960–1969	1970–1979	1980–1983
Total	–32	–47	–38
Through agricultural price policies	–8	–15	–3
Through other public policies[b]	–24	–32	–35

Source: Federico (2005: 203).
Notes: [a] Argentina, Brazil, Chile, Colombia, Dominican Republic, Egypt, Ghana, Ivory Coast, Malaysia, Morocco, Pakistan, Philippines, Portugal, South Korea, Sri Lanka, Thailand, Turkey and Zambia.
[b] Includes the direct impact of other agricultural policies (for instance, public investment in the sector) and the indirect impact of non-agricultural policies (for instance, industrial and exchange rate policies).

TABLE 3.6 Product composition of exports from developing countries (%)

	Food and agricultural raw materials	Minerals, metals and fuels	Manufactured products
1912	78	14	8
1938	69	22	9
1953[a]	57	33	10
1970[a]	37	47	16
1980[a]	15	66	19
1990[a]	16	34	50

Source: Bairoch (1997, III: 925).
Note: [a] Only countries with a market economy.

world wars) had contributed to this pessimistic mood, but the latter also had deeper roots: the sensation that the orientation towards agricultural exports in previous historical periods had not led to successful development results.

All of this reinforced a trend that would have probably unfolded anyway, considering the South's pattern of specialization in products the demand for which was not very expansive on an international level (Serrano and Pinilla 2016): the economies of the South ceased to be the kind of agri-exporting economies that they had been during the nineteenth century and the early part of the twentieth century. In fact, after the Second World War, exports from the South became strikingly more diverse (Table 3.6), and the link between exports and economic growth became much weaker than it had been in the past – for instance, prior to the First World War (for Latin America, see Martín-Retortillo et al. 2018: 346, 353). Under these conditions, the consolidation of European protectionism through the CAP could not have the devastating impacts that have often been suggested by fierce critics.

Finally, it is not even clear that a different European policy, one more compatible with the South's agri-exporting efforts, would have made that much of a difference when it comes to fighting world poverty. Critics of the distortions induced by the North's policies do not go too deep into the issue of what would really happen if said distortions were eliminated (Andersson and Rohne Till 2018: 33). Previous historical experiences in the South illustrate the fragility of the chain of effects that goes from growth in agricultural exports, on one end, to poverty reduction, on the other. Critics of the CAP tend to assume a simple, self-evident connection between both ends, but history suggests a different lesson. In the nineteenth and early twentieth centuries, many countries and colonies had economies based on the export of agricultural products to developed countries, at a time when the latter had only moderately protectionist trade policies (or even free trade policies). However, with the exception of the "new Europes" of North America and Oceania, almost all of these economies failed to achieve remarkable results in development and poverty reduction. Sustaining the growth of agricultural exports was not always an easy task, partly due to endogenous problems, partly due to the changing conjunctures of global markets for each particular product. Moreover, sustained growth in exports did not guarantee that a structural transformation involving an increase in the economy's growth potential (for instance, a process of industrialization) would begin. Furthermore, the benefits of agricultural exports were commonly reaped by a small number of landowners who controlled the domestic markets for land and labour. As a result, agri-export growth could take place alongside persistent pockets of rural poverty and marginality (Bulmer-Thomas 2003: Chapters 3–5; Gunnarsson 2018; Pinilla and Willebald 2018: 19–23).

Some of these problems are, in fact, being experienced once again in the last few decades by some countries in the global South. Their economic policies have already corrected their anti-agrarian bias, and agricultural exports have grown rapidly. New products, such as fresh fruits, vegetables and also raw materials for animal feed, play a prominent role in this (Martín-Retortillo et al. 2018: 352–357). Additionally, this happens at a time when successive reforms of the CAP have moderated both agricultural protectionism and direct export subsidies, creating a more favourable environment for the agri-exporting reorientation of the South. But, once again, the link between export-led growth and poverty reduction is not obvious (Akram-Lohdi and Kay 2009; Gunnarsson 2018). The return of agri-export growth has actually put the "agrarian question" and distributional tensions back in the policy agenda of many countries, especially in Latin America (Botella 2018). In a complementary way, international institutions such as the Food and Agricultural Organization have insistently called governments to reorient their policy agenda towards family farmers producing for the domestic market as a more effective way to fight rural poverty than pursuing export-led growth (McMichael 2013: 154).

Let us take for instance the case of the great dynamism experienced in the last few years by Latin America's exports of soy into the European market. Apparently, this is the kind of agri-export growth that the classic CAP would have unfortunately hampered for too long a time. And, yet, a closer examination of this growth model suggests that it is not inclusive enough from both a social and an environmental point of view. Agri-export interests have been recurrently accused of threatening family farmers producing for the domestic market and of inducing rapid deforestation (Fritz 2012: 94–111). Marxist sociologists and anti-globalization activists also blame the European model of agriculture for this. It is after all the

European livestock farming sector that demands Latin American soy and triggers the aforementioned sequence of events. However, when some problems arise if the EU does one thing as well as if it does the opposite thing, it becomes difficult to assign the EU such a central role in the analysis. Agricultural exports past and present have never been a panacea, allegedly ruined by the CAP and other similar policies of the global North.

The heart of the matter is that, contrary to what neoclassical economists often imply, it is not at all evident that liberal capitalism is the optimal arrangement. Let us take the "ACP countries" (Africa–Caribbean–Pacific) as a contrast case. Most of these are former colonies of EU member states (especially France) and their agricultural sectors are oriented towards products that for the most part are not in direct competition with European interests. Thanks to their early incorporation into what would eventually become the EU's policy of development cooperation, ACP countries have been able to benefit from preferential access to the European market. In fact, from the 1990s onwards their access has become almost completely unrestrained. They have a clear surplus in their agri-food trade balance with the EU. However, after decades of having benefited from the kind of trade relationship with the EU that allegedly would have been so positive for all of the global South, it seems clear that, on its own, liberalization has not been the highly effective lever of growth (not to say development) that many critics of the CAP have taken for granted it would be (Lingard and Hubbard 1997; Andreosso-O'Calaghan 2003: 201).

Active public policies are required in order to promote family farming and strengthen food-industry clusters. As a matter of fact, a comparison of the disparate experiences of different African countries highlights the relevance of domestic policy decisions in this area (Fritz 2012: 95–97). However, many of the countries in the South (especially in Latin America and Africa) failed to seize the window of opportunity that was opened in the decades after the Second World War, precisely when the EEC implemented the CAP in the context of a much broader shift towards coordinated capitalism (Koning 2017: Chapter 5). For the South, the later turn towards the market, which has substantially reduced the room for the design and application of active public policies, is not necessarily the great news that critics of the CAP have always suggested it would be (Chang 2009).

Conclusion

The CAP has generated impacts and costs. For a long time, it has forced Europeans to spend more money on their food. Past and present, it has been financed by the EU budget: in its absence, the European taxpayer would not have had to pay so many taxes or would have seen some reallocation of public expenditure towards other, more inclusive ends. Finally, the CAP has harmed some interests outside the EU: agricultural protectionism has prevented other countries from exporting more, and export subsidies have weakened the (already weak) food systems of more than a few countries in the global South.

This chapter has argued, however, that these impacts have been (and are) more modest than is commonly suggested. The extra prices paid by European consumers were not very high, especially when considered in the context of the making of a mass consumer society in which the share of food expenditure decreased substantially. The fiscal burden imposed on European taxpayers by the CAP has been insignificant if we position it within the bigger picture of the making of welfare states. Finally, it is unlikely that, leaving aside some very specific exceptions, the global South would have fared much better had the EU had an agricultural policy of different, or even opposed, characteristics.

In all cases, furthermore, the negative impacts of the CAP have become milder as time has gone by. The paradigm change started by the MacSharry reform in 1992 and consolidated by the Fischler reform in 2003 reduced the gap between agricultural prices in Europe and the wider world, contained the budget cost of the CAP, and phased out the policy instrument that was more detrimental to the interests of poorer countries (export subsidies). If at some point in the 1980s the CAP could have been feared to become a monster out of control (which, for the reasons discussed in this chapter, was an exaggeration), the reforms of the last quarter century have definitively removed that possibility.

The criticisms that have been raised by neoclassical economists and Marxist sociologists, among others, exaggerate the magnitude and relevance of the impacts generated by the CAP. This partly reflects their adherence to disputable assumptions, such as taking allocative efficiency as the main criteria for the evaluation of public policies (in the case of neoclassical economists) or taking for granted that the trajectory of the South can be explained mostly by the policies implemented in the North (in the case of Marxist sociologists). It also reflects a different way of interpreting the available empirical evidence, as well as (more importantly) of fitting diverse pieces of evidence within a single historical account.

But, does this mean that we should make a positive assessment of the CAP? Obviously not. It just means that its negative aspects should not be overstated. But, what about the positive side? Does the CAP incarnate the alleged virtues of European-style coordinated capitalism? Has it contributed to social and territorial cohesion, as well as to environmental sustainability? That is the topic of the next chapter.

References

Ackrill, R. 2000. *The Common Agricultural Policy*. Sheffield: Sheffield Academic Press.

Akram-Lohdi, A. H. and Kay, C. 2009. "Neoliberal globalization, the traits of rural accumulation and rural politics: The agrarian question in the twenty-first century". In *Peasants and globalization: Political economy, rural transformation and the agrarian question*, eds. A. H. Akram-Lohdi and C. Kay, 315–337. London: Routledge.

Andersson, M. and Rohne Till, E. 2018. "Between the engine and the fifth wheel: An analytical survey of the shifting roles of agriculture in development theory". In *Agricultural development in the world periphery: A global economic history approach*, eds. V. Pinilla and H. Willebald, 29–61. London: Palgrave Macmillan.

Andreosso-O'Callaghan, B. 2003. *The economics of European agriculture*. Basingstoke: Palgrave Macmillan.

Aparicio, G., Pinilla, V., and Serrano, R. 2009. "Europe and the international trade in agricultural and food products". In *Agriculture and economic development in Europe since 1870*, eds. P. Lains and V. Pinilla, 52–75. Abingdon: Routledge.

Aparicio, G., González-Esteban, Á. L., Pinilla, V., and Serrano, R. 2018. "The world periphery in global agricultural and food trade, 1900–2000". In *Agricultural development in the world periphery: A global economic history approach*, eds. V. Pinilla and H. Willebald, 63–78. London: Palgrave Macmillan.

Ash, R., Du, J., and King, C. 2018. "Perspectives on agricultural and grain output growth in China from the 19th century to the present day". In *Agricultural development in the world periphery: A global economic history approach*, eds. V. Pinilla and H. Willebald, 307–334. London: Palgrave Macmillan.

Bairoch, P. 1993. *Economics and world history: Myths and paradoxes*. Chicago: University of Chicago Press.

Bairoch, P. 1997. *Victoires et déboires: histoire économique et sociale du monde du XVIe siècle à nos jours*. Paris: Gallimard.

Booth, A. 2018. "Southeast Asian agricultural growth: 1930–2010". In *Agricultural development in the world periphery: A global economic history approach*, eds. V. Pinilla and H. Willebald, 235–255. London: Palgrave Macmillan.

Botella, E. 2012. "El modelo agrario costarricense en el contexto de la globalización (1990–2008): oportunidades y desafíos para reducir la pobreza rural". *Ager* 12: 7–49.

Botella, E. 2018. "La cuestión agraria en América Latina: desafíos recurrentes y nuevas preguntas para la historia rural". In, *Del pasado al futuro como problema: la historia agraria contemporánea española en el siglo XXI*, eds. D. Soto and J. M. Lana, 285–311. Zaragoza: Prensas Universitarias de Zaragoza.

Bulmer-Thomas, V. 2003. *La historia económica de América Latina desde la independencia*. México: Fondo de Cultura Económica.

Chang, H.-J. 2009. "Rethinking public policy in agriculture: Lessons from history, distant and recent". *Journal of Peasant Studies* 36 (3): 477–515.

Cipolla, C. M. 1974. *The economic history of world population*. London: Penguin.

Cipolla, C. M. 1991. *Allegro ma non troppo*. Barcelona: Crítica.

Collantes, F. 2017. *La economía española en 3D: oferta, demanda y largo plazo*. Madrid: Pirámide.

Collantes, F. and Pinilla, V. 2011. *Peaceful surrender: The depopulation of rural Spain in the twentieth century*. Newcastle-upon-Tyne: Cambridge Scholars Publishing.

Cunha, A. and Swinbank, A. 2011. *An inside view of the CAP reform process: Explaining the MacSharry, Agenda 2000, and Fischler reforms*. Oxford: Oxford University Press.

Etzioni, A. 2016. "The next industrial revolution calls for a different economic system". *Socio-Economic Review* 14 (1): 179–183.

European Commission. 2009. *EU budget 2008: Financial report*. Luxembourg: Office for Official Publications of the European Communities.

Federico, G. 2005. *Feeding the world: An economic history of world agriculture, 1800–2000*. Princeton: Princeton University Press.

Fritz, T. 2012. *Globalizar el hambre: impactos de la Política Agrícola Común (PAC) y de las políticas comerciales de la UE en la soberanía alimentaria y los países del Sur*. Madrid: ACSUR-Las Segovias, Ecologistas en Acción, Plataforma 2015, Plataforma Rural, Veterinarios sin Fronteras and Asociación Trashumancia y Naturaleza.

Gardner, B. 1996. *European agriculture: Policies, production and trade*. London: Routledge.

González-Esteban, Á. L. 2017. "Why wheat? International patterns of wheat demand, 1939–2010". *Investigaciones de Historia Económica* 13 (3): 135–150.

González-Esteban, Á. L. 2018. "Patterns of world wheat trade, 1945–2010: The long hangover from the second food regime". *Journal of Agrarian Change* 18 (1): 87–111.

Gunnarsson, C. 2018. "Ghana's recurrent miracle: Cocoa cycles and deficient structural change". In *Agricultural development in the world periphery: A global economic history approach*, eds. V. Pinilla and H. Willebald, 121–151. London: Palgrave Macmillan.

Judt, T. 2005. *Postwar: A history of Europe since 1945*. London: Penguin.

Koning, N. 2017. *Food security, agricultural policies and economic growth: Long-term dynamics in the past, present and future*. London: Routledge.

Lingard, J. and Hubbard, L. 1997. "The CAP and the developing world". In *The Common Agricultural Policy*, eds. C. Ritson and D. R. Harvey, 343–357. Wallingford: CAB International.

McMichael, P. 2013. *Food regimes and agrarian questions*. Winnipeg: Fernwood.

Malassis, L. 1997. *Les trois âges de l'alimentaire. Essai sur une histoire sociale de l'alimentation et de l'agriculture, II: L'âge agro-industriel*. Paris: Cujas.

Martín-Retortillo, M., Pinilla, V., Velazco, J., and Willebald, H. 2018. "The goose that laid the golden eggs? Agricultural development in Latin America in the 20th century". In *Agricultural development in the world periphery: A global economic history approach*, eds. V. Pinilla and H. Willebald, 337–363. London: Palgrave Macmillan.

Milward, A. S. 2000. *The European rescue of the nation-state*. London: Routledge.

OECD. 2017. *Agricultural support estimates – 2017 edition*, https://stats.oecd.org.

Patel, K. K. 2009. "Europeanization *à contre-cœur*. West Germany and agricultural integration, 1945–1975". In *Fertile ground for Europe? The history of European integration and the Common Agricultural Policy since 1945*, ed. K. K. Patel, 139–160. Baden-Baden: Nomos.

Pinilla, V. 2018. "Agricliometrics and agricultural change in the nineteenth and twentieth centuries", working paper DT-AEHE-1803.

Pinilla, V. and Serrano, R. 2009. "Agricultural and food trade in the European Union, 1961–2000". In *Fertile ground for Europe? The history of European integration and the Common Agricultural Policy since 1945*, ed. K. K. Patel, 273–300. Baden-Baden: Nomos.

Pinilla, V. and Willebald, H. 2018. "Agricultural development in the world periphery: A general overview". In *Agricultural development in the world periphery: A global economic history approach*, eds. V. Pinilla and H. Willebald, 3–27. London: Palgrave Macmillan.

Pinilla, V. and Willebald, H. (eds.) 2018. *Agricultural development in the world periphery: A global economic history approach*. London: Palgrave Macmillan.

Pollan, M. 2008. *In defense of food: An eater's manifesto*. New York: Penguin.

Popkin, B. M. 1993. "Nutritional patterns and transitions". *Population and Development Review* 19 (1): 138–157.

Pujol, J. and Cussó, X. 2014. "La transición nutricional en Europa occidental, 1865–2000: una nueva aproximación". *Historia Social* 80: 133–155.

Ritson, C. 1997. "The CAP and the consumer". In *The Common Agricultural Policy*, eds. C. Ritson and D. R. Harvey, 241–264. Wallingford: CAB International.

Schwartz, B. 2004. *The paradox of choice: Why more is less*. New York: Harper.

Serrano, R. and Pinilla, V. 2016. "The declining role of Latin America in global agricultural trade, 1963–2000". *Journal of Latin American Studies* 48 (1): 115–146.

Skidelsky, R. and Skidelsky, E. 2012. *How much is enough? Work, money and the good life*. London: Penguin.

Swinnen, J. 2018. *The political economy of agricultural and food policies*. New York: Palgrave Macmillan.

Tracy, M. 1989. *Government and agriculture in Western Europe, 1880–1988*. New York: New York University Press.

4

AN EVEN GREATER MYTH

Coordinated agrarian capitalism

Precisely at the time when EU institutions were beginning to talk insistently about the so-called European model of agriculture, geographer Henry Buller (2001: 2) wrote, "[The] European model is essentially a series of broad policy objectives, most of which are still far from being achieved". Almost twenty years later, can this opinion be sustained? Is the CAP an agricultural incarnation of the alleged virtues of coordinated capitalism? Or, rather, is the European model merely a rhetorical artefact set to make the CAP more legitimate in the eyes of public opinion and third countries?

This chapter organizes the answer to these questions in three sections. The first explores the main argument that has been made to justify the CAP: the need for a policy that, in line with the broader conception of a welfare state, supports farmers' income in order to get them closer to the rest of the citizens. While the farm-income problem has been alluded to from the very beginning of the CAP, other dimensions were brought about by the debate on the European model of agriculture in the 1990s. These are considered in the other two sections of the chapter. The second section examines the environmental consequences of the CAP, while the third section assesses the degree to which this policy has contributed to the socio-economic development of Europe's rural communities.

An agricultural welfare state?

CAP advocates are right that farmers are, from a socio-economic point of view, a vulnerable occupational group. Farmers are vulnerable in the short run, because agricultural production is always under the threat of downward fluctuation as a result of climatological events, plagues and other undesired circumstances. Perhaps more crucially, farmers are also vulnerable in the longer term because in modern economies farm income tends to remain persistently below the income level

TABLE 4.1 Relative productivity of agricultural labour (average labour productivity in the national economy = 100)

	1960	1980	2008	2017
France	36	50	57	65
Germany	36	50	55	51
Italy	42	45	54	59
Poland			21	23
Spain		41	65	71
United Kingdom		67	55	43

Sources: Ambrosius and Hubbard (1989: 58–59); Prados de la Escosura (2003: 591–595); Mitchell (2007: 1036–1043); Eurostat (ec.europa.eu/eurostat, *National accounts*).

prevailing in the rest of the occupations. The root of this income gap is that the average farmer is remarkably less productive than the average worker in the rest of the industrial sectors.

This is a stylized fact that we find in nearly all past and present economies for which data are available. European economies are no exception. Around the early 1960s, when the CAP began to be implemented, the relative productivity of agriculture was strikingly low all across the EEC (Table 4.1). Today, in spite of impressive agricultural growth propelled by technological change and efficiency gains (Martín-Retortillo and Pinilla 2015), agricultural productivity remains remarkably low in comparison to productivity in the other sectors of the respective national economies. On average, agricultural productivity today is hardly one-third of the average productivity of the EU economy (calculated from Eurostat, <ec.europa.eu/eurostat>, *National accounts*).

The causes of low agricultural productivity are diverse. Partly, farmers are less productive than other occupational groups because farming has a lesser technological content than other activities. Even though many innovations have been introduced, particularly during the last century, technological change has been even greater in manufacturing and some service activities (Freeman and Louçã 2001). Partly, the problem for farmers has to do with the prices at which markets value their output. The demand for agricultural products is less dynamic than that for industrial products and services. This is particularly problematic for farmers living in affluent societies, where consumers have their basic nutritional needs met already (Malassis 1997). Finally, the low productivity of agriculture also reflects, especially in historical contexts, that farming often absorbs underemployed labour that, in the absence of employment opportunities in manufacturing or services, remains attached to the family farm (Simpson 1995).

It is true that the income gap between farming and the rest of the occupations is commonly lower than the productivity gap. Farmers do not lag behind the other occupational groups as much as productivity data would suggest. Farmers live in rural areas where consumer prices are lower than in the cities, so that their

TABLE 4.2 Relative farm income (average of the national economy = 100)

	2008	2015
Western European member states	53	54
Central and Eastern European member states	37	50

Source: European Commission (2017a).

purchasing power is not as low as it may seem. Moreover, they have the chance to resort to the self-consumption of products coming from their own farm. Their patrimony, furthermore, may be based on housing and land property to a greater extent than that of many urban families. Finally, farmers past and present are commonly multi-active workers who are simultaneously involved in several different activities. Today, most farmers are actually part-time farmers who earn most of their income from non-farm pursuits.

These and other nuances make the measuring of farmers' relative income a technically complex area, where small differences in statistical categories may provoke noteworthy differences in results (Hill 2011). Some evidence, for instance, suggests that the farm-income gap has tended to diminish and that it may have even disappeared around 1990 (Harvey 1997: 178–183; Federico 2005: 212–213). Other works, however, find a persistent gap (Malassis 1997: 303–306; Koning 2017: Chapter 7). This second possibility probably fits better with the perceptions of political actors and social stakeholders during the era of the classic CAP (Knudsen 2009: 267–275; Lovec 2016: 80). For the reformed CAP, it also fits with the official statistics prepared by the European Commission, which show that a remarkable farm income gap has persisted until today (Table 4.2).

CAP advocates argue that this policy has contributed to mitigating the farm income problem. Are they right? In a way, they are. The most common indicator in this area is the ratio between "producer subsidy equivalent" and farm income. As explained in Chapter 2, this allows us to learn the proportion of farm income that comes from subsidies and other public support. Figure 4.1 shows that, in relation to the national policies that were in force in each country prior to the 1960s, the CAP implied a clear increase in public support to farm incomes (see also Federico 2009: 263–264, and Spoerer 2015: 204–205). The classic CAP, with its mechanisms for market intervention, injected income into farmers' pockets by an amount of more than 40 per cent of their gross income.

It is true that this value has been decreasing over the last quarter century, most markedly after the turn of the millennium. This would seem to speak poorly of the CAP's recent results in social terms, but two important details must be kept in mind. First, the fall in agricultural support (thus measured) could be consistent with an income gap that today is likely to be somewhat smaller than it was a few decades ago. The relative productivity of agriculture remains low, but has increased modestly. As long as this has been transmitted (wholly or, more plausibly, partially) to farmers'

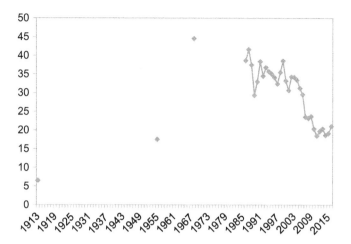

FIGURE 4.1 Public support of European farmers as a percentage of farm income

Sources: 1913-1968 (approximate dates and levels): Federico (2011: 123, 130-131); 1986-2016: OECD (2017).

incomes, a decreasing level of public support may be consistent with a narrowing farm income gap.

And, second (and more important), the indicator we are using is very sensitive to changes in world agricultural prices and changes in the policies of large commercial blocks such as the EU. More specifically, the gradual phasing out of the EU's export subsidies has exerted an upward pressure on world prices, as the practice of dumping large quantities of agricultural produce at artificially low prices has been abandoned. In addition, the last decade has been a period of surprisingly high prices in agricultural world markets, as a consequence of factors such as the demand pull coming from emerging economies, land-use competition between food and (bio-)fuels, and the impact of speculative fluctuations in the agri-finance subsector. These high prices have increased farm incomes and, therefore, have made EU public support look smaller in relative terms (Anderson et al. 2013).

Even so, around one-fifth of European farmers' income would still depend on public support – a figure far from negligible. CAP advocates are right when they argue that, in the absence of subsidies, the farm income gap would be even greater. It is hard to exaggerate what this means for a multitude of small farmers with low incomes. For them, the CAP is a vital complement of the national policies of the welfare state. This is especially clear among elderly farmers who lack any prospect of making a successful move to other activities. Judt (2011: 22) is clearly going too far when he states that "the CAP [...] never benefited a majority of peasants".

The fallacy of the argument about the CAP as an agricultural welfare state, however, lies in mistaking this part for the whole. The CAP cannot be truly put on the same level as the social protection policies of the welfare state because its benefits have always been distributed in a tremendously uneven way. Most of the support given by the classic CAP was absorbed by a small number of farmers: those with the

TABLE 4.3 Distribution of direct payments according to their amount (%)

	2002		2016	
	Beneficiaries	*Payments*	*Beneficiaries*	*Payments*
Less than 500 euros	55	4	27	1
500 to 1,250 euros			24	3
1,250 to 5,000 euros	24	12	26	11
More than 5,000 euros	21	84	23	85
Total	100	100	100	100

Source: European Commission (2017b).

largest farms, the highest level of capitalization and the strongest technological base (Knudsen 2009: 273). It was they who were able to benefit most from the market interventions run by the EEC. It was they, for instance, who were able to produce sizeable surpluses and then sell them to the EEC at profitable intervention prices. It was also large business units, especially large corporations in the food and trade sectors, that became the main beneficiaries of export subsidies (Gardner 1996: 30–31). In other words, even though the classic CAP benefited all actors in the sector, it benefited the largest actors the most. Commissioner MacSharry spoke in the early 1990s of an "80/20 unbalance": 80 per cent of the classic CAP's resources were absorbed by not more than 20 per cent of beneficiaries, while 80 per cent of farmers had to share out the remaining 20 per cent of farm support (Gardner 1996: 51; Ackrill 2000: 209).

Even though some researchers have suggested that the post-1992, reformed CAP has become more re-distributional (Knudsen 2009: 3, 297), the pattern of inequality in the distribution of farm support has not really changed much (Table 4.3). The MacSharry reform, for instance, did not have any chance of correcting the 80/20 unbalance because it coupled farm subsidies to the number of hectares and live-stock units on the farm. As a matter of fact, what this reform did was to secure a transition from support via prices to support via payments that would be more or less neutral in distributional terms. In the 1990s, internal-control institutions such as the European Court of Auditors consequently accused the CAP of not fulfilling its declared social justice objective because of its lack of focus on vulnerable and unprofitable farms (Cardwell 2004: 64).

Partly in response to this, the idea of introducing some "degressivity" in farm support began to spread among EU policymakers. During Franz Fischler's double term, in particular, some social modulation of farm support was introduced – first optionally for member states and later on in a compulsory way. But, beyond rhetoric, this modulation has been extraordinarily feeble. The subsidies going to large farmers only become proportionately smaller beyond a very high threshold, if they ever do at all (Table 4.4). In other words, the CAP does not do anything in order to reduce inequality within the farming community.

TABLE 4.4 Decisions by the largest member states in relation to capping the subsidies perceived by the largest farmers (2014–2020)

	Is there any capping?	How much?	Beyond what threshold?
Germany	No		
Spain	Yes	5%	150,000 euros
France	No		
Italy	Yes	50%	150,000 euros
Poland	Yes	100%	150,000 euros
United Kingdom	Yes	30%, 55% and 100%	200,000, 250,000 and 300,000 euros

Source: European Commission (2015: 18).

TABLE 4.5 Percentage of direct payments and land in the hands of the 20 per cent of largest beneficiaries and farmers, 2015

	European Union	France	Germany	Italy	Poland	Spain	United Kingdom
Payments	82	54	69	80	74	78	64
Land	82	53	71	76	66	81	69

Source: European Commission (2017b).

What MacSharry termed the 80/20 unbalance (a very effective illustration that has been regrettably left behind in the public debate on the CAP) remains standing, then. Still, today, there is a clear correspondence between the degree of concentration on land property and the degree of concentration on farm subsidies in EU countries (Table 4.5). To make matters worse, in many countries the elite of large-subsidy beneficiaries has frequently included high-level politicians, many belonging to the agri-policy network in which CAP decisions are made (Compés 2006; Fritz 2012: 36–40; Segrelles 2017).

The CAP: an agricultural welfare state? What would we think of our retirement pension system if 4 per cent of the retirees were absorbing half of the total public expenditure made in pensions? The CAP may be a welfare-state policy for a majority of small farmers, but it is not even remotely so when it is seen as a whole. The support given to farmers is not sufficiently focused on those who need it the most, while it flows abundantly to well-off social groups and large organizations.

A "green" policy?

CAP advocates are right that farming is a part of the environmental problem that Europe and the wider world are currently facing. In fact, it is a surprisingly large part of the problem. In the decades after the Second World War, there was a rapid transition towards agricultural systems that were much more productive than were the traditional counterparts, but also much more polluting. Traditional farming did not have much of an impact on the environment because it would rely on organic energy sources, closely linked to the cycles and rhythms of the natural world. Furthermore, much of its waste would be used again as an input for production at a later stage; for instance, animal manure would be recycled as a soil fertilizer. In contrast, modern farming makes intensive use of fossil fuels: it is based on tractors and other machines and requires many external inputs (i.e. chemical fertilizers) to be transported to the countryside. Moreover, modern farmers are more specialized, so that they have less opportunity to recycle the waste coming from some productions into inputs for other ones; for instance, for the owner of an intensive poultry farm, in which raising chickens is the only activity and in which chickens are given industrial feed (instead of natural feed coming from pastures and meadows cultivated by the farmer), manure is just an inconvenient waste material. This has made modern farming become an activity with strong impacts on the atmosphere, the soils and the waters (McNeill 2000; González de Molina et al. 2017).

To this we must add a related impact: the impact on landscapes. CAP advocates are right that there may be a link between keeping some farming activity in a region and preserving its landscape quality. Partly as a consequence of the aforementioned technological changes, partly as a consequence of the spread of new opportunities to work and live in cities, large areas that were previously under cultivation or used for livestock have been abandoned. The result has been a less-harmoniously coordinated land-use pattern, the dismantling of traditional agrarian landscapes, and the start of spontaneous processes of reforestation of little environmental value (Collantes and Pinilla 2011: 133–135).

But, are those who argue that the CAP has been helping us fight these problems right? Again, they partly are. During the last 20 years, and as we have read in Chapter 2, the criteria for granting subsidies have gradually incorporated an environmental dimension. In consequence, the CAP has been moving farmers to adopt practices that are more environment-friendly, such as extensification and crop diversification. In the absence of public intervention, these changes may well have not been taking place.

The environmental effects of decoupled subsidies must also be taken into account. The fact that subsidies have been increasingly decoupled from production has probably made a major contribution to one of the most remarkable facts of Europe's recent agricultural history: the end of a long wave (starting around 1945) of rapid growth in the use of chemical fertilizers and tractors (Houpt et al. 2010: 336–339; Martín-Retortillo and Pinilla 2015: 144–145). This has been good for the environment because it has reduced the impact of farming on the soils, the waters and the atmosphere.

It is also likely that, in the absence of public intervention, the abandonment of agricultural areas would have been even more drastic. After all, the economic support granted by the CAP may have allowed many extensive farms to become more viable. In the absence of public intervention, structural adjustment in the agricultural sector would have been even more severe (Federico 2005: 214–215), as it would have been the associated deterioration of landscapes in many areas.

And yet the environmental outcome of the CAP is actually quite poor. To begin with, the classic CAP, which lacked any environmental criterion in its design, contributed to accelerating farmers' transition towards industrial, high-pollution agriculture. Under the classic CAP, support was completely coupled to production, so the bigger the latter, the bigger the former. Therefore, the classic CAP gave farmers incentives to produce as much as possible in order to maximize the public support coming from market intervention. This included incentives to adopt all innovations that would allow them to increase their output, irrespective of environmental impacts. The use of tractors and chemical fertilizers would have probably increased rapidly anyway, but the CAP gave an additional boost to the process (Lowe and Whitby 1997; Martín-Retortillo and Pinilla 2015: 144–145). Without the CAP, many farmers would have decided to produce less or, at the margin, to abandon their farms. Farming would have become an intensive, industrialized activity anyway, but its scale (and, therefore, its environmental impact) would have remained smaller. On the other hand, the pro-export bias of the classic CAP was detrimental for the environment as well, since it promoted long-distance trade and, therefore, greenhouse gas emissions.

This is the context in which the contribution of later reforms to a more sustainable agriculture must be positioned. In part, what the reforms have done is, simply, to create incentives for farmers to take some steps back down the path that the classic CAP had actually encouraged them to follow (Figure 4.2). Moreover, change is happening very slowly, as a comparison between farming and the rest of the economy shows (Table 4.6). While agriculture's share in GDP decreases rapidly,

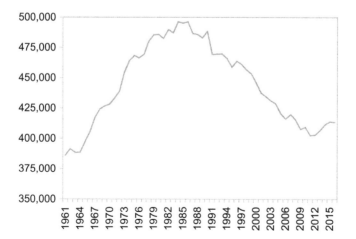

FIGURE 4.2 Greenhouse gas emissions by agriculture in the European Union (gigagrams of carbon dioxide equivalents)

Source: Faostat (www.fao.org/faostat, *Emissions-Agriculture*).

TABLE 4.6 Pollution intensity of European agriculture

	1995	2005	2015
Share in greenhouse gas emissions (%)	8.7	8.2	9.8
Share in GDP (%)	2.4	1.5	1.4
Pollution intensity[a]	3.6	5.5	7.0

Sources: Emissions in 1995: Faostat (www.fao.org/faostat, *Agri-environmental indicators*); rest of data: Eurostat (ec.europa.eu/eurostat, *Agri-environmental indicators* and *national accounts*).
Note: [a] Ratio between agriculture's share in greenhouse gas emissions and its share in GDP; the average of the economy has a pollution intensity of one.

TABLE 4.7 Percentage of the utilized agricultural area devoted to organic farming

	European Union	France	Germany	Italy	Poland	Spain	United Kingdom
2000		1.2	3.2	6.7	0.2[a]	1.5	3.3
2007	4.0	1.9	5.1	7.9	1.8	4.0	3.7
2016	6.7	5.3	6.8	14.0	3.7	8.5	2.8

Source: Eurostat (ec.europa.eu/eurostat, *Agri-environmental indicators*).
Note: [a] 2003.

its share in total greenhouse gas emissions is today larger than 20 years ago. In relative terms, farming has become an ever-bigger part of the European environmental problem.

To what extent has the reformed CAP been able to go beyond simply dismantling the most perverse part of its incentive structure? To what extent has it succeeded in promoting a "post-productivist" transition (Ilbery and Bowler 1998) that moves us away from mainstream industrial farming? The answer is not much. Organic agriculture has been growing but remains a marginal practice (Table 4.7). Successive CAP reforms have introduced environmental criteria for the granting of subsidies, but they have done so in a very soft way. The environmental conditionality of the late 1990s and early 2000s was just an attempt to correct the most striking excesses of productivist agriculture. It penalised a number of farming practices that were openly damaging for the environment, but it did not provide incentives for farmers to transition towards an alternative model (Cardwell 2004: 189–194). Incentives of that kind could be found in (some of) the agri-environmental measures contained in the CAP's second pillar, but this was a very small share of CAP expenditure and, therefore, could have but a modest impact on the overall trends of European agriculture. In 2008, the European Court of Auditors reached a radical conclusion: the alleged environmental turn of the CAP had actually been a sham (Compés 2010: 145; cf. Koning 2017: 164).

The last round of CAP "greening", which has led to the current regime of "green payments", has allowed member states to introduce positive environmental incentives within the first pillar, but with little success. Most states have opted for a very relaxed definition of the requisites that farmers need to meet in order to realize the green payment (López García 2012). A strict definition could have restricted the receipt of the green payment to organic farmers. Being an organic, truly alternative farmer, however, is just one of the many ways in which the green payment can be cashed in. The green payment has rapidly become a payment on which most farmers can count in spite of not being involved in any substantial reorientation of their practices. The European Court of Auditors (2017) estimates that green payments have not induced any reorientation in as much as 95 per cent of the EU's farmland, and the court therefore remains unconvinced about the potential of this instrument (as it is currently defined) to enhance the environmental performance of European agriculture.

This confirms the pessimistic forecast made in the 1990s by the first generation of researchers who studied agri-environmental measures: whenever there is tension between environmental objectives and the objective of supporting farm income, the latter overcomes (Lowe and Whitby 1997; Ortiz Miranda and Ceña 2002). It is likely that in the future we will see the CAP taking further steps towards the promotion of sustainable farming, but what we have seen by now is mostly a missed chance. It is discourse, rather than actual reality, that becomes greener.

A pillar of rural development?

CAP advocates cannot be blamed for stressing that Europe has a problem of territorial cohesion and that rural areas are an important part of it. In almost every EU country, both population and economic activity are concentrated in a few metropolitan areas. Many rural areas, conversely, find much trouble retaining their population numbers and keeping their business network dynamic.

It is true that it is simplistic to pose this as a dichotomy. There is not one single type of rural area. Some districts have witnessed (and are witnessing) extreme processes of depopulation that not only are intrinsically painful, but also lead to a rapidly aging rural society that lacks the human capital and entrepreneurial spirit necessary to bring about a change in its own decadent trajectory. Other areas have certainly experienced a forceful revitalization that has involved a reactivation of hidden sources of economic dynamism and the attraction of new residents. This has been linked to both endogenous initiatives and the spread to the countryside of exogenous business projects and life plans (Collantes and Pinilla 2011: Chapters 5 and 9). Nor are cities and metropolitan areas all the same. Some fit well with the classical image of urban dynamism, as reflected in the renovation of their productive structures and in rising population numbers. Others, however, are facing decline issues that are not very different from those that many rural areas have been dealing with for a long time now: crisis in their traditional economic base (manufacturing, in particular) and demographic decline (Wolff and Weichman 2017). In fact, the very distinction between urban and rural areas is not as useful as it used to be. There are, for instance, many areas that were originally rural but have become incorporated with the residential peripheries of nearby urban areas. Partly because of that, the economic, material and human flows between different types of geographical spaces have intensified, dissolving much of the meaning of traditional categories such as "urban society" and "rural society" (Camarero 2009).

Even so, rural decline remains an important threat to territorial cohesion in most parts of Europe. In Western European countries such as the United Kingdom, France, Italy or Spain, the most severe stage of rural depopulation has been left behind: the era of mass rural–urban migrations came to a close sometime during the twentieth century (most commonly, sometime between around 1970 and the 1990s) and rural areas, considered as a whole, are actually experiencing a slight increase in their population numbers (Collantes and Pinilla 2011: Chapter 1). Yet, many local and regional cases of rural depopulation persist. Whole regions of Spain and Scandinavia display extremely low population densities and do not have any clear prospects of reversing the trend. In the meantime, the pace of rural depopulation has become remarkable in Central and Eastern Europe, especially in countries such as Romania and Poland (Collantes and Pinilla 2011: Chapter 1). In any of these cases, most rural population perceive their socio-economic problems from a territorial point of view (that is, as rural problems) and much of the broader public opinion agrees that some public intervention is needed in order to promote rural development.

CAP advocates are also right when they point out that some of the policies implemented by the EU have exerted a positive impact in that direction. A very good example is the LEADER initiative, which started out in the 1990s.

initiative, which started out in the 1990s as an autonomous policy instrument implemented by the European Commission and became a part of the CAP in 2007. Generally speaking, these rural development plans, designed by local action groups, have been fairly successful on their own terms. When it comes to the local economy, LEADER has channelled public and private investments towards those activities that have the highest potential to retain population in rural areas: non-farm activities. As a large body of evidence past and present shows, depopulation tends to hit hardest where the rural economy remains strongly dependent on agriculture, while demographic recovery only takes place where a diversified local economy emerges (Collantes 2004, 2009). This result was to be expected, considering the farm income gap that we have dealt with earlier in this chapter. Seen from this angle, LEADER has not only promoted rural development, but has done so in the right direction in order to fight population decline: shifting the focus from agriculture to the rest of the rural economy.

LEADER's balance, on the other hand, is not bad in social and political terms either. In many cases, the initiative has revitalized the decadent, fatalist social atmosphere legated by depopulation (Buciega 2013). It has also implemented a new model of territorial governance, with an enhanced role for civil society. It is true that in this area reality has lagged behind discourse. Almost from the beginning, local political elites in the most backward regions (in Southern Europe in particular) managed to play roles that should have been played by civil society members. Something similar seems to be happening more recently with national and regional bureaucracies, as LEADER has become incorporated with the CAP, and these bureaucracies have emerged as intermediaries between Brussels and the local action groups (Esparcia et al. 2015; Navarro et al. 2016). These qualifications notwithstanding, LEADER clearly has one of the most positive outcomes within the whole of the CAP (Granberg et al. 2015).

However, we should not forget that LEADER has always had a very modest level of funding. In its beginnings, it was just a pilot project, implemented in a few dozen European districts. Today, and in spite of the fact that repeatedly positive evaluations from the Brussels establishment have secured LEADER a stable, consolidated position, it does not absorb more than a very small share of the expenditure made on CAP's second pillar, which in turn is a small share of total CAP expenditure. In other words, LEADER may have gone in the right direction, but its power to change the trajectory of rural economies has been severely limited. Needless to say, most of the new opportunities for rural employment that have flourished in the last few decades have done so independently of LEADER. The variety of cases is astonishing, going from rural economies transformed by their incorporation into nearby industrial districts to rural economies rapidly shifting to service-sector specialization after the arrival of new residents. In comparison with this array of market forces, very unevenly present across the European countryside, LEADER has been just a secondary complement in the right direction.

The CAP's overall balance in the area of rural development is mediocre, actually. Its advocates argue that the CAP contributes to rural development because it attaches agricultural populations to the villages, and because farm support may contribute at a later stage to the development of other rural activities, for instance food processing. Both claims, however, are based on a crude distortion of reality.

Does CAP not contribute to attaching farmers to the countryside? Does it not improve the viability prospects for farmers who would otherwise abandon the rural areas? This is a very biased way of tackling it. The first question we should pose is: does farming really contribute to attaching population to rural areas? And the answer, backed by a large body of evidence for different countries and historical periods (Collantes 2004, 2009; Collantes and Pinilla, 2011: Chapter 10), is a resounding no. Farming has retained population in the countryside only as long as European economies have remained industrializing economies incapable of creating abundant employment opportunities in manufacturing and services. Once these opportunities are created (as has been the case throughout all of the historical period covered by the CAP), farming becomes unable to retain significant population numbers. The farm income gap is too large, even inside each rural community.

Farmers have in fact become a minority group within their own rural communities. In rural Europe today, most of GDP and employment are contributed by the non-farm sectors, while agriculture is of secondary importance (Table 4.8). All across Europe, a striking "de-agrarianization" of rural societies has taken place over the last

TABLE 4.8 Share of agricultural gross added value (GAV) and employment in rural areas[a] (%)

	EU	France	Germany	Italy	Poland	Spain	United Kingdom
2002							
GAV	5.7	6.0	3.7	4.5	5.8	9.0	6.2
Employment	14.2	7.9	6.4	8.6	27.6	15.9	8.4
2016							
GAV[b]	4.2	3.9	2.0	5.0	6.4	7.4	3.9
Employment	13.5	5.0	3.5	7.2	22.8	11.4	6.3

Sources: 2002: European Commission (2006: 40–41); 2016: European Commission (ec.europa.eu, *Agriculture*, "CAP context indicators – 2017").
Notes: [a] "Predominantly rural" NUTS-3 territories (OECD criteria). This definition of rurality is crude because it leaves out the rural areas in highly urbanized provinces and does not exclude the cities of the more rural provinces. However, these two bias seem to cancel out one another in large measure; see for instance the similarity between the figures in this table and the more rigorous figures given by García Sanz (2011: 127, 391) for the particular case of rural Spain.
[b] 2014.

half century (or more, in the British case). In some cases, those of the more dynamic rural areas, "de-agrarianization" has been fostered by business development in new sectors, such as manufacturing, construction and tourism. It has also been favoured by the incorporation of rural areas to urban real estate markets and the subsequent arrival of new dwellers (mostly, urban middle classes delinked from farming or traditional rural life), as well as by their positive impact on the local service sector. These cases have been very unevenly distributed across rural Europe, but it is interesting to note that, in the absence of rural dynamism, it is depopulation that stimulates the "de-agrarianization" of rural societies. There where the rural economy was not diversifying beyond agriculture, mass farm out-migration towards the cities would transform the rural occupational structure, making it become dominated by non-farm pursuits with more power to retain population. In consequence, traditional rural society, seen as a society where farmers and farming is the backbone, has disappeared in both the dynamic and the declining areas (Collantes 2009).

Furthermore, in some historical periods the path of technological change followed by agriculture leads it to lose population, rather than retain it. This is particularly the case of European agriculture under the classic CAP. In part following the incentives provided by the CAP, farmers enthusiastically invested in labour-saving innovations (i.e. tractors) that increased their potential output while simultaneously making much labour redundant (Bairoch 1999; Martín-Retortillo and Pinilla 2015). This was not necessarily bad, as the labour power released from agriculture often had a good chance of shifting to other, more remunerative activities. But, of course, the post-1945 pattern of agricultural growth, reinforced by the CAP's incentive structure, favoured rural depopulation, especially where (as was the case in most of Europe) rural economies lacked a strong non-farm sector capable of absorbing the farmers and agricultural labourers pushed out by agrarian change. The classic CAP, however, did not pay any attention to the diversification of rural economies or the prevention of depopulation.

How much have things changed during the long era of reforms that started in 1992 and continue to the present? After all, the reformed CAP has included territorial criteria in several aspects of its design. Most visibly, since 1999 the CAP comprises, alongside its first pillar of farm subsidies, a second pillar that is supposed to be about rural development. This second pillar, however, has been barely effective and for a number of reasons. To begin with, its level of funding has always been low – much lower than that of the first pillar (Figure 4.3). From very early on, doubts were raised within EEC institutions that the second pillar had enough funding to effectively fight rural marginalization trends (Cardwell 2004: 221). Moreover, the second pillar has always suffered from chaotic internal organization. It has always been a hodgepodge in which several different generations of policy instruments, ranging from those coming from the structural policy of the 1970s to the new ones created by the latest round of reform, were put together without any kind of integrating principle or vision (Castillo and Ramos 2010). It is not at all clear that rural development funds have been allocated in a way that is in accord with the heterogeneous circumstances of the different European regions (Lovec 2016: 129).

Even more importantly, a fundamental problem is that most second-pillar funds are systematically misallocated to ends that are not economic diversification or the promotion of the rural quality of life. The second pillar is called rural development, but this is a very imperfect description of what it really does. As we saw in Chapter 2, it comprises many measures that actually belong to other areas, such as

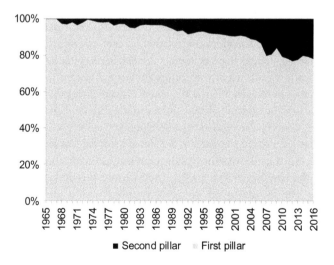

FIGURE 4.3 Shares of the first and second pillars in CAP expenditure (%)

Sources: 1965-1999: European Commission (2009: 77-81); 2000-2016: European Commission (<ec.europa.eu>, *Budget,* "EU expenditure and revenue 2014-2020").

TABLE 4.9 Breakdown of second pillar expenditure according to type of measure (%)

	2000–2006	2007–2013	2014–2020
Farm competitiveness	38	36	30[a]
Agri-environmental measures	52	46	52
Rural economy and society[b]	10	18	15

Sources: 2000–2006: European Commission (2003: 5); 2007–2013: Directorate-General for Agriculture and Rural Development (2011: 268); 2014–2020: European Commission (ec.europa.eu, *Agriculture*, "Rural development programs 2014–2020").

Notes: [a] Includes food chain organization, animal welfare and risk management.
[b] Promotion of economic diversification and rural quality of life.

subsidies set to improve farmers' competitiveness (a classic instrument coming from the structural policy of the 1970s) or subsidies that provide incentives for farmers to transition to sustainable practices (an instrument that has its roots in the agri-environmental measures of the early 1990s).

As a matter of fact, farm subsidies of one kind or another have persistently absorbed most of the CAP expenditure that is officially devoted to "rural development" (Table 4.9). There is a large variety of national and regional situations, since it is actually up to each member state to manage the allocation of their second pillar funds (Lowe et al. 2002; Rosell et al. 2010). All generalization must proceed cautiously then, but there are only a few exceptions of regional governments who have chosen economic diversification, rural quality of life and LEADER as the main axis of their second pillar. In most cases, what prevails is the use of second pillar funds to complement the farm subsidies of the first pillar (Table 4.10). Some countries, like Spain and Poland, are focused on pro-competitiveness subsidies. Others, like France, Germany and most prominently the United Kingdom, are focused on agri-environmental subsidies. No doubt these subsidies may perhaps be useful for tackling real problems such as the farm income gap or the unsustainability of European farming, but for the reasons exposed (see also Colino and Martínez Paz 2005; and Collantes 2010) they are not effective when it comes to fighting depopulation and promoting the economic development of rural areas. The second pillar is called rural development, but it is really no such a thing.

But, perhaps, subsidising farmers is a way of creating linkages with the non-farm sectors and thus promoting rural economic diversification? Perhaps farm subsidies are the base upon which a local food-processing industry (for instance) may flourish? The answer, again, seems to be no. It is not just that farmers (as we have seen) are a very small part of the rural population today, but also that farming's power to stimulate the development of non-farm activities seems to be very small nowadays. Many studies of the economic geography of the food chain, for instance, show that decisions about business location are less and less related to the location of raw materials (for a review, see Collantes 2016). Other, more generic, determinants of business location matter more; among them, seizing the external economies made possible by pre-existing industrial clusters (where there

TABLE 4.10 Breakdown of second pillar expenditure according to type of measure in the largest member states (%), 2007–2013

	Farm competitiveness	Agri-environmental measures	Rural economy and society
France	33	57	10
Germany	28	44	28
Italy	39	45	16
Poland	43	33	24
Spain	46	42	12
United Kingdom	12	77	11

Source: Directorate-General for Agriculture and Rural Development (2011: 268).

is better access to technologies, information and other inputs) or getting close to large concentrations of potential consumers. Accordingly, the key to the geography of the food industry seems to lie at the regional level rather than at the purely local one. This does not mean that the food-processing industry cannot contribute to rural development. What it means is that it cannot at all be taken for granted that subsidising farmers in a given district will be the first step towards food industrialization in that district.

In summary, the image of the CAP as an incarnation of the alleged virtues of European-style "coordinated capitalism", which we have already found problematic in its social and environmental dimensions, is not tenable in territorial terms either.

Conclusion

The idea that the CAP has allowed the EU to shape some sort of coordinated agrarian capitalism is purely rhetorical. The CAP is not a proper welfare-state policy because it is not designed according to an equality criterion and mostly benefits large farmers and large companies. Nor is the CAP a green policy, because it has induced remarkable environmental impacts and today it just gives a few weak, minor incentives for farmers to transition to a truly sustainable technological model. Finally, the CAP is not a pillar of rural development because most of the funds it is supposed to devote to that end (which are not many) are actually diverted to other purposes. CAP's triple fiasco portrays a great myth – that of coordinated agrarian capitalism in the framework of the "European model of agriculture".

Rather than coordinated agrarian capitalism, what we find is a failure to coordinate Europe's agrarian capitalism according to the values exposed by the policymakers and largely shared by public opinion. The reasonable degree of public support that the CAP repeatedly gets in the Eurobarometers reflects the Commission's success during the last half century when it comes to positioning this policy within a constellation of political values that are shared by most EU citizens. However, it also reflects the degree to which citizens are unable to perceive the wide gap that has always existed, and exists, between the Commission's discourse and CAP's actual reality.

This, in its turn, fits with a broader implication of the general debate on the European economic and social model: the need to tell discourses and values, on the one hand, from actual reality, on the other. It is dubious that Europe has a distinctive agricultural model (as was examined in Chapter 2), but it is an even greater distortion to argue that the CAP embeds the values of social justice, environmental sustainability and territorial cohesion that it is supposed to be defending. This is in line with the arguments by sociologists and geographers who, in the last two decades, have questioned the European model of agriculture from premises that are not at all hostile to the notion of coordinated capitalism. It is also in line with those economists who have doubted that the CAP has implemented the policy instruments that are truly required in order to solve the market failures that, from their theoretical viewpoint, would justify some public intervention in the farming sector.

The question that comes next is: why, then, do we have this agricultural policy in Europe? Why, in particular, this missed opportunity in terms of coordinating capitalism? Today as in the past, the Commission's changing discourse tries to make the CAP legitimate in the eyes of European public opinion and (more recently) third countries, but it cannot be taken as an explanation of the real reasons why the CAP is the way it is. In order to identify those reasons, the next chapter shifts the focus from the socio-economic to the political.

References

Ackrill, R. 2000. *The Common Agricultural Policy*. Sheffield: Sheffield Academic Press.

Ambrosius, G. and Hubbard, W. H. 1989. *A social and economic history of twentieth-century Europe*. Cambridge: Harvard University Press.

Anderson, K., Rausser, G. and Swinnen, J. 2013. "Political economy of public policies: Insights from distortions to agricultural and food markets". *Journal of Economic Literature* 51 (2): 423–477.

Bairoch, P. 1999. *L'agriculture des pays dévelopées de 1800 à nos jours: production, productivité, rendements*. Paris: Economica.

Buciega, A. 2013. "Capital social y LEADER: los recursos generados entre 1996 y 2006". *Ager* 14: 111–144.

Buller, H. 2001. "Is this the European model?". In *Agricultural transformation, food and environment: perspectives on European rural policy and planning*, eds. H. Buller and K. Hoggart, 1–8. Aldershot: Ashgate.

Camarero, L. 2009. "Introducción". In *La población rural de España: de los desequilibrios a la sostenibilidad social*, coord. L. Camarero, 9–17. Barcelona: La Caixa.

Cardwell, M. 2004. *The European model of agriculture*. Oxford: Oxford University Press.

Castillo, J. S. and Ramos, E. 2010. "El nuevo desarrollo rural y el futuro de la política rural en la Unión Europea". In *"Chequeo médico" de la PAC y perspectivas de la Política Agraria Común tras 2013*, coords. J. M. García Álvarez-Coque and J. A. Gómez Limón, 177–212. Madrid: Eumedia and Ministerio de Medio Ambiente y Medio Rural y Marino.

Colino, J. and Martínez Paz, J. M. 2005. "El desarrollo rural: segundo pilar de la PAC". In *Política agraria común: balance y perspectivas*, coords. J. L. García Delgado and M. J. García Grande, 70–99. Barcelona: La Caixa.

Collantes, F. 2004. *El declive demográfico de la montaña española (1850–2000): ¿un drama rural?* Madrid: Ministerio de Agricultura, Pesca y Alimentación.

Collantes, F. 2009. "Rural Europe reshaped: The economic transformation of upland regions, 1850–2000". *Economic History Review* 62 (2): 306–323.

Collantes, F. 2010. "Exit, voice, and disappointment: Mountain decline and EU compensatory rural policy in Spain". *Public Administration* 88 (2): 381–395.

Collantes, F. 2016. "Places in common: Exploring the economic geography of the food system through the case of Spain's dairy chain". *TSEG – The Low Countries Journal of Social and Economic History* 13 (4): 17–40.

Collantes, F. and Pinilla, V. 2011. *Peaceful surrender: The depopulation of rural Spain in the twentieth century.* Newcastle-upon-Tyne: Cambridge Scholars Publishing.

Compés, R. 2006. "Los principios básicos de la reforma 'intermedia'". In *La reforma de la Política Agraria Común: preguntas y respuestas en torno al futuro de la agricultura*, coord. J. M. García Álvarez-Coque, 35–60. Madrid: Eumedia and Ministerio de Agricultura, Pesca y Alimentación.

Compés, R. 2010. "De la deconstrucción a la refundación: elementos para un cambio de modelo de reforma de la PAC 2013". In *"Chequeo médico" de la PAC y perspectivas de la Política Agraria Común tras 2013*, coords. J. M. García Álvarez-Coque and J. A. Gómez Limón, 129–153. Madrid: Eumedia and Ministerio de Medio Ambiente y Medio Rural y Marino.

Directorate-General for Agriculture and Rural Development. 2011. *Rural development in the European Union: Statistical and economic information. Report 2011.* Brussels: European Commission.

Esparcia, J., Escribano, J. and Serrano, J. J. 2015. "From development to power relations and territorial governance: increasing the leadership role of LEADER Local Action Groups in Spain". *Journal of Rural Studies* 42: 29–42.

European Commission. 2003. *Overview of the implementation of rural development policy 2000–2006: Some facts and figures.* Luxembourg: Office for Official Publications of the European Communities.

European Commission. 2006. *Rural development in the European Union: Statistical and economic information. Report 2006.* Luxembourg: Office for Official Publications of the European Communities.

European Commission. 2009. *EU budget 2008: Financial report.* Luxembourg: Office for Official Publications of the European Communities.

European Commission. 2015. *Direct payments post 2014: Decisions taken by Member States by 1 August 2014.* Brussels: European Commission.

European Commission. 2017a. "CAP post-2013: key graphs and figures", https://ec.europa/agriculture.

European Commission. 2017b. "Facts and figures on EU agriculture and the CAP (Direct payments)", https://ec.europa.eu/agriculture.

European Court of Auditors. 2017. "Greening: a more complex income support scheme, not yet environmentally effective", Special Report no. 21.

Federico, G. 2005. *Feeding the world: an economic history of world agriculture, 1800–2000.* Princeton: Princeton University Press.

Federico, G. 2009. "Was the CAP the worst agricultural policy of the 20th century?". In *Fertile ground for Europe? The history of European integration and the Common Agricultural Policy since 1945*, ed. K. K. Patel, 257–271. Baden-Baden: Nomos.

Federico, G. 2011. *Breve historia económica de la agricultura.* Zaragoza: Prensas Universitarias de Zaragoza and Institución Fernando el Católico.

Freeman, C. and Louçã, F. 2001. *As time goes by: From the industrial revolutions to the information revolution.* Oxford: Oxford University Press.

Fritz, T. 2012. *Globalizar el hambre: impactos de la Política Agrícola Común (PAC) y de las políticas comerciales de la UE en la soberanía alimentaria y los países del Sur.* Madrid: ACSUR-Las Segovias, Ecologistas en Acción, Plataforma 2015, Plataforma Rural, Veterinarios sin Fronteras and Asociación Trashumancia y Naturaleza.

García Sanz, B. 2011. *Ruralidad emergente: posibilidades y retos.* Madrid: Ministerio de Medio Ambiente y Medio Rural y Marino.

Gardner, B. 1996. *European agriculture: Policies, production and trade.* London: Routledge.

González de Molina, M., Soto, D., Infante-Amate, J., Aguilera, E., Vila, J., and Guzmán, G. I. 2017. "Decoupling food from land: the evolution of Spanish agriculture from 1960 to 2010". *Sustainability* 9: 2348.

Granberg, L., Andersson, K., and Kovách, I. 2015. "Introduction: LEADER as an experiment in grass-roots democracy". In *Evaluating the European approach to rural development: Grass-roots experiences of the LEADER programme*, eds. L. Granberg, K. Andersson and I. Kovách, 1–12. Abingdon: Routledge.

Harvey, D. 1997. "Extensions and political analysis of the CAP". In *The Common Agricultural Policy*, eds. C. Ritson and D. R. Harvey, 163–190. Wallingford: CAB International.

Hill, B. 2011. *Understanding the Common Agricultural Policy.* London: Routledge.

Houpt, S., Lains, P., and Schön, L. 2010. "Sectoral developments". In *Cambridge economic history of modern Europe, vol. 2: 1870–2000*, eds. K. H. O'Rourke and S. Broadberry, 333–359. Cambridge: Cambridge University Press.

Ilbery, B. and Bowler, I. 1998. "From agricultural productivism to post-productivism". In *The geography of rural change*, ed. B. Ilbery, 57–84. Essex: Longman.

Judt, T. 2011. *A grand illusion? An essay on Europe.* New York: New York University Press.

Knudsen, A.-C. L. 2009. *Farmers on welfare: The making of Europe's Common Agricultural Policy.* Ithaca, NY: Cornell University Press.

Koning, N. 2017. *Food security, agricultural policies and economic growth: Long-term dynamics in the past, present and future.* London: Routledge.

López García, D. 2012. "La reforma de la PAC 2014–2020: más mercado, más miseria y menos agricultores/as". In *Globalizar el hambre: impactos de la Política Agrícola Común (PAC) y de las políticas comerciales de la UE en la soberanía alimentaria y los países del Sur*, T. Fritz, 4–12. Madrid: ACSUR-Las Segovias, Ecologistas en Acción, Plataforma 2015, Plataforma Rural, Veterinarios sin Fronteras and Asociación Trashumancia y Naturaleza, pp. 4–12.

Lovec, M. 2016. *The European Union's Common Agricultural Policy reforms.* London: Palgrave Macmillan.

Lowe, P., Buller, H. and Ward, N. 2002. "Setting the next agenda? British and French approaches to the second pillar of the Common Agricultural Policy". *Journal of Rural Studies* 18 (1): 1–17.

Lowe, P. and Whitby, M. 1997. "The CAP and the European environment". In *The Common Agricultural Policy*, eds. C. Ritson and D. R. Harvey, 285–304. Wallingford: CAB International.

McNeill, J. R. 2000. *Something new under the sun: An environmental history of the twentieth-century world.* New York: Norton.

Malassis, L. 1997. *Les trois âges de l'alimentaire. Essai sur une histoire sociale de l'alimentation et de l'agriculture, II: L'âge agro-industriel.* Paris: Cujas.

Martín-Retortillo, M. and Pinilla, V. 2015. "Patterns and causes of the growth of European agricultural production, 1950 to 2005". *Agricultural History Review* 63 (1): 132–159.

Mitchell, B. R. 2007. *International historical statistics: Europe 1750–2005.* Basingstoke: Macmillan.

Navarro, F., Woods, M., and Cejudo, E. 2016. "The LEADER initiative has been a victim of its own success: The decline of the bottom-up approach in rural development programmes. The cases of Wales and Andalusia". *Sociologia Ruralis* 56 (2): 270–288.

OECD. 2017. *Agricultural support estimates – 2017 edition*, https://stats.oecd.org.

Ortiz Miranda, D. and Ceña, F. 2002. "Efectos de la política agroambiental de la Unión Europea en el mundo rural". *Información Comercial Española* 803: 105–118.

Prados de la Escosura, L. 2003. *El progreso económico de España (1850–2000)*. Bilbao: Fundación BBVA.

Rosell, J., Viladomiu, L., and Correa, M. 2010. "Mejora del medio ambiente y nivel de desarrollo: las opciones de los Programas de Desarrollo Rural (2007–2013) de la Unión Europea". *Revista Española de Estudios Agrosociales y Pesqueros* 226: 13–37.

Segrelles, J. A. 2017. "Las ayudas agrarias y sus repercusiones sobre la agricultura familiar en la última reforma de la Política Agraria Común (2014–2020) de la Unión Europea: ¿cambiar para que todo siga igual?". *Boletín de la Asociación de Geógrafos Españoles* 74: 161–183.

Simpson, J. 1995. *The long siesta: Spanish agriculture, 1765–1965*. Cambridge: Cambridge University Press.

Spoerer, M. 2015. "Agricultural protection and support in the European Economic Community, 1962–92: Rent-seeking or welfare policy?". *European Review of Economic History* 19: 195–214.

Wolff, M. and Wiechmann, T. 2017. "Urban growth and decline: Europe's shrinking cities in a comparative perspective 1990–2010". *European Urban and Regional Studies* 25 (2): 122–139.

5

THE POLITICAL BACK ROOM

As economist Allan Buckwell (1997: 141) points out, in the case of the CAP "the best explanation for today's policy is always yesterday's policy". That is why in this chapter, in which we will search for the political origins of the CAP, we will continue to apply a historical approach. Considering the conclusions of the preceding chapters, we are interested in giving an answer to two questions. First, why has the CAP been a missed chance in terms of coordinated capitalism? Why has its policy process been deformed, reducing the CAP's potential in social, environmental and territorial terms? And, second, why has the CAP not become an out-of-control monster? What are the correcting mechanisms that have deactivated the main problems of the original CAP?

The chapter is organized in four sections. The first provides the conceptual framework that will be used throughout the rest of the chapter. The second section analyses the policy process of the original CAP and shows how the balance of interests achieved by the EEC, member states and farm organizations drove the CAP away from the social problems it was meant to act upon. The third section explains the internal and external pressures that in the late 1980s destabilized this balance of interests, giving way to the important reforms that during the last quarter century have corrected some of the worst dysfunctionalities of the classic CAP. The fourth section, finally, analyses the political reasons why these reforms have not gone too far in social, environmental or territorial terms. The conclusions in the fifth section reflect on the tension between continuity and change in the CAP's political back room.

From rational choice to historical institutionalism

Why do governments, especially in developed countries, support farmers? An influential explanation is rooted in rational-choice theory, a field in which economists and political scientists live together under the epistemological premises of neo-classical economics. Their core proposal is that public policies result from an equilibrium between interest groups that lobby politicians for decisions that will have a positive impact on their income, on the one hand, and politicians who make their policy decisions on the basis of optimizing their electoral support and career prospects, on the other (Swinnen 2018).

In the influential account by economist and political scientist Mancur Olson (1990), for instance, the key lies in the success of farm interest groups when it comes to influencing policymakers, so that the latter implement farm-support policies. Farm organizations would be particularly effective because, contrary to other interest groups, they represent a relatively small number of people, because these people share fairly homogeneous interests, and because the costs of communication within this small, united group are low. This would allow farm organizations to focus on a small number of clearly defined policy objectives and lobby politicians accordingly.

On the other hand, from the viewpoint of politicians, it would be rational to take into consideration the demands made by farm interest groups. In doing so, politicians secure the social and electoral support of farmers, on which the benefits of the policy are concentrated. What about the costs of the policy? Precisely because farmers are few, costs can be diluted among a large mass of taxpayers and consumers for whom agricultural matters are not a prime concern. In consequence, applying agricultural support policies maximizes the level of social and electoral support achieved by politicians, who thus get closer to their objective of remaining in office and making progress in their career. This transaction between farm organizations and policymakers could lead to a very stable equilibrium, making agricultural policy strongly path-dependent. More specifically, it is unlikely that politicians implement reforms that attack agricultural interests. In that case, they would be causing direct harm to a well-defined, well organized group. Farmers' political support would be lost, and the minor, diluted benefits accruing to the rest of society would not be able to compensate for that.

Within this framework, the "developmental pattern" hypothesis suggests that it is not by chance that developed countries support farmers more strongly than poor countries (Lindert 1991). Neither is it a paradox that farmers benefit from more generous support policies where they are less in number. It is precisely the relative decline of agriculture in modern society that would create conditions favourable to the making of solid, successful interest groups, especially because of the small size of the population represented by said groups. It would also create conditions favourable for politicians to dilute the cost of supporting farmers among a large mass of taxpayers and consumers, who are mostly uninterested in the agricultural-policy debate. Prior to reaching some threshold of development, however, farm interest groups would not be so effective, and politicians would have to consider more carefully other interests, in particular consumer interests (see also Olson 1990, and for the particular case of the CAP, Spoerer 2015).

This hypothesis, however, is just a one-off theoretical observation and it can explain just a part of the changes that can be identified empirically. An alternative, more inclusive conceptual framework is that of historical institutionalism, which focuses on the temporal processes and events that have an influence on the origin and trajectory of the institutions and policies involved in the regulation of social relations (Fioretos et al. 2016). This framework, epistemologically closer to the political-economy approach of this book, has been used to analyse the causes of agricultural policies in developed countries by political scientists such as Sheingate (2001) and Kay (2006: 90–103) as well as by historians such as Knudsen (2009a, 2009b). Sheingate, in particular, has argued that the theoretical world of rational choice only portrays well a very specific phase in the contemporary history of agricultural policies: the decades after the Second World War, when agricultural policies in places as different from one another as the United States, France and Japan, embodied a clientelist relationship between farm organizations and the government.

In previous or later periods, however, other variables would have to be incorporated, including the political system, the institutional structure, the organization pattern of governments and political parties, the higher or lower degree of executive power in the hands of governments, or the definition of the "policy venue" in which agricultural policy decisions are made. As a matter of fact, in Sheingate's interpretation these variables also contribute to explaining even the clientelist policies of the postwar period, emerging thus as conditional causes that had remained omitted in rational-choice models (see also Fernández 2016). A second, more recent generation of rational-choice models has actually been paying more attention to these political variables, while acknowledging that the influence and initiative of interest groups had probably been given too prominent a role in previous accounts (de Gorter and Swinnen 2002; Anderson et al. 2013).

In terms of our analysis, the major implication of historical institutionalism is that it invites us to consider the conditions under which clientelist policies may be reformed (or even dismantled), overcoming the inertia involved in the transaction between farm interest groups and policymakers. Sheingate takes from political scientist James Q. Wilson the notion of "entrepreneurial politics" and makes it central to his analysis of the pressures to reduce farm support – pressures that spread across much of the developed world in the late twentieth century. True: clientelist politics creates inertia, but it also creates conditions favourable for the emergence of political entrepreneurs, that is, politicians who take the risk of attacking vested interests and mobilize other interests that are more diffuse but potentially massive. The strategy of entrepreneurial politicians would be to try to change the policy venue, so that interests other than those of farmers, such as those of taxpayers, consumers or ecologists, are incorporated into the decision-making process.

Their degree of success at achieving this depends much on circumstances. In principle, we would expect political entrepreneurs to be more successful in contexts in which the farming community is ideologically fragmented, the internal organization of political parties is loose, and it is possible to offer compensations to the groups harmed by policy reform. However, if farmers are perceived as the electoral patrimony of one of the major parties, if said parties are organized in a rigid way that leaves little room for manoeuvre to its individual members, and if no credible, tangible compensations can be offered to the potential losers from policy change, then it is much less likely that political entrepreneurs would be successful – or that they even exist at all.

The focus of historical institutionalists on the tension between inertia leading to policy continuity, on the one hand, and forces that may potentially disrupt the existing political equilibrium, on the other, creates an open-ended analytical framework that can account for diverse empirical trajectories, ranging from paradigm shift to minor adjustments within relatively stable paradigms or the lack of any substantial change at all. The stress on path dependency favours the adoption of a chronological explanation (as will be the case in the remainder of this chapter), but that stress does not imply a deterministic account in which the power of inertia necessarily overcomes any potentially disruptive forces.

The original sin

A common agricultural policy had the potential to illustrate the virtues of European-style coordinated capitalism. The Treaty of Rome identified a series of social problems related to farming: low agricultural productivity, fluctuations in farm incomes, low living standards among the farming community, the need to ensure food supplies at reasonable prices for the rest of the population. It is true that some of these objectives were quickly relegated in both discourse and practice, while others, especially the one related to food security, were already anachronistic at the time they were formulated (Eichengreen 2007: 182). But the objective of improving the living standard of farmers, in particular, was repeatedly emphasised in the discourse of EEC institutions.

Why, then, was not the original CAP a true agricultural welfare state, strongly oriented towards social justice? Basically, because the policy process was deformed by other interests and objectives from very early on (Hill 2011). These other interests and objectives were not opposed or incompatible with the ones defended by the Treaty of Rome, but they were different, indeed. Therefore, they contributed to shaping the CAP in a different direction. The farm-income problem was important in order to justify the CAP, but never became crucial to its design and implementation. The design of the original CAP actually resulted from the political equilibrium that was reached among three major actors: member states, the EEC and farm organizations. In relation to the two political vertices of this triangle, it is striking the degree up to which both European and national policymakers interpreted the CAP as a policy the main value of which was not intrinsic as much as it was instrumental. The issue was not solving the farm-income problem as much as it was using that problem to create a supranational economic policy that contributed to the political consolidation of the European integration project.

The integration project required its promoters to identify areas in which common interests could be pursued by means of supranational policies and institutions, but this was not so easy. Agriculture was a more plausible choice than other areas because the founding member states had more or less similar backgrounds in terms of their domestic policies: increasing state intervention in agricultural markets during the world wars and their interlude and, in most cases, the increasing influence of farm organizations in the design and implementation of public policies. During the years between the end of the Second World War and the creation of the CAP, national agricultural policies had evolved along broadly similar lines, positioning the farm-income problem as their raison d'être and favouring market intervention as the main policy instrument (Tracy 1989: Chapter 11; Milward 2000: 225–253; Knudsen 2009a: 23–56; Brassley et al. 2016). By then, the agricultural political elites of each country had begun to rely, to some extent, on economic growth as an instrument that would smooth distributional tensions, as had also been the case with economic policy elites more broadly (Schmelzer 2016). It was simpler to reach intergovernmental agreements in this area than in others in which national policies were more dissimilar.

In addition, there was also a core of pro-agrarian values that were widely shared by policymakers and citizens (Knudsen 2009b). For some, the issue was to defend a reserve of cultural traditions that were constitutive of the national identity. For others, the issue was to extend to the countryside the values of social cohesion and welfarism that were becoming dominant during the postwar decades. In any case, there was a favourable predisposition towards public initiatives that would support farmers. Probably, the drastic socio-economic changes that took place during the postwar decades, such as the acceleration of industrialization and the rise of mass consumers and urban middle classes (de Grazia 2005), contributed to making these pro-agrarian values even more solid than they already were.

Once first-level political negotiations about the EEC identified agriculture as the best area in which a common European policy could be created, second-level negotiations about the CAP became strongly conditioned by the high instrumental value that policymakers from both the member states and the new EEC institutions attached to reaching some agreement on the matter. In other words, reaching an agreement was more important than fighting for the perfect agreement. Of course, this was positive in a way, as the comparison between the CAP and its frustrated predecessor, the Green Pool of the 1950s, shows. In both cases, the negotiations between member states were full of tension – an inevitable reflection of national interests that were different and that sometimes could even be antagonistic. However, the Green Pool negotiations, disconnected from a broader agenda of European integration, concluded without any tangible results (Thiemeyer 2009). The negotiations over the CAP, conversely, were successful because participants found incentives to eventually moderate their positions. For the Federal German Republic, for instance, the project of CAP that was being discussed was problematic. It was doubtful that this was the best possible policy for Europe, and it certainly was not the best policy for Germany, as German taxpayers would be forced to subsidize any productivist excesses of the French agri-food sector. But European integration promised great potential benefits to the EEC's major industrial power. Within the German government, the pro-CAP position of the chancellor and the minister of agriculture eventually prevailed over the anti-CAP position of the minister of economy (Patel 2009).

However, the fact that CAP negotiations were successful due to instrumental considerations deformed the policy process. The design of the CAP was influenced by a number of factors that had little (or nothing at all) to do with the previous phase of problem identification. Quickly, negotiations came to be focused on the most convenient way of Europeanizing the clientelist agricultural policies that member states were already applying on their own (Milward 2000: 224–317). For France, the essential point was that its farmers, especially the large cereal farmers from the North, remained able to find consumers for an output that was evidently growing faster than domestic demand and traditional foreign demand. For the Federal German Republic, the essential point was that its farmers remained able to sell their output at prices that were at least similar to those that until then had been made possible by the national agricultural policy. This meant prices that were substantially higher than those prevailing in the other five member states. For the Netherlands, the essential point was to implement a truly common policy of market intervention, instead of simply creating a common market for farmers who would have different levels of national support as a result of different national intervention policies. Negotiations over the CAP were successful because participants were able to find a balance among these three positions: a common market for agricultural products, regulated by a common policy of market intervention based on high guaranteed prices.

But what was left of the discussion on the most effective means to fight the problem that was supposed to motivate the whole policy process – that is, the farm-income gap? What was the best way of supporting farmers? Compensating their low level of income with public transfers? And, if so, was it better to do it with market interventions or with direct payments? With sector-wide instruments or with instruments that were focused on small, low-income farmers? Or perhaps it was better to fight the underlying problem, that is, the structural shortcomings that prevented farmers from being as productive as workers in other sectors? And, if so, to what extent should the EEC promote a structural adjustment that would push thousands of very small, uncompetitive farmers out of agriculture, so that those who remained in the sector had larger and better farms?

None of these questions seems to have at all bothered national agricultural policymakers and negotiators. This is striking not only in itself, but also inasmuch as it reveals a complete lack of interest on the part of member states in assessing the results of their own pre-CAP agricultural policies. By the time the intergovernmental negotiations over the design of the original CAP started, a number of technical reports (among them, but not exclusively, those authored by the OECD) were available questioning that price policies were truly effective for correcting the farm-income problem (Knudsen 2009a: 48–55, 211–212).

The important question about how exactly farmers should be supported was not openly ignored by the EEC. The first agriculture commissioner, Sicco Mansholt, agreed that correcting the farm-income problem had to be the main objective, but remained unsatisfied about the original design of the CAP. Mansholt thought that it provided perverse incentives for the continuity of the least competitive part of European agriculture. The farm-income problem resulted from an underlying productivity gap, but the original CAP was not designed to make farmers more productive. In fact, only a few years later Mansholt published a controversial report in which he recommended a less-generous price policy and a substantial transfer of CAP funds to structural measures that allowed farmers to become more competitive. However, during the negotiations leading to the creation of the CAP, Mansholt did not fight hard to defend this alternative to the Europeanized clientelist policy that member states were shaping. Once immersed in the clientelist paradigm, Mansholt does not even seem to have employed all of the potential for technical consulting that was available to him in order to be more influential on issues such as the choice of support instruments (Knudsen 2009a: 146–148). Similar to national politicians, the EEC commissioner also seemed to attach a great instrumental value to reaching some agreement on the CAP, and this moved him to temporally relativize any intrinsic problems that the agreement could suffer from (van Merriënboer 2009).

The confluence of member states and EEC politicians needed, finally, to be in tune with the third vertex of a triangle: farm organizations. In all countries, farm organizations had become a stable, reliable channel of contact between the state and rural civil society. In fact, during the half century prior to the creation of the CAP, farm organizations not only had become more powerful as pressure groups that had an influence on political decisions, but also as collaborators of the state in the implementation and management of public policies (Lanero 2018: 264). In the decades after the Second World War, moreover, a combination of institutional, socio-economic and political factors made farm organizations particularly relevant.

In the institutional sphere, it has to be noted that in the two key countries for the negotiation of the original CAP, France and Germany, the representation of farm interests was concentrated on a large organization that had close ties with government: the DBV (German acronym for German Farmers' Association) and the FNSEA (in French, National Federation of Farmers' Associations). The subsequent Europeanization of agricultural policy made these ties even stronger, as national governments and farm organizations had the challenge of negotiating in an effective course in front of the other governments and organizations (Milward 2000: 237–241; Sheingate 2001: 161–176). The policy community was so used to relying on farm organizations as interlocutors and co-managers that the European Commission spurred the creation of a European-level organization to work with: the Committee of Professional Agricultural Organisations (COPA) (Patel 2009: 149). Similar to what its national counterparts had been doing prior to European integration, COPA eventually played a key role as a co-manager of the original CAP alongside the European Commission and the European Council. By spreading the EEC's mainstream messages on the farm-income problem and market intervention, COPA was also important when it came to making the CAP more legitimate in the eyes of European farmers (Knudsen 2009a: 263, 312; Cunha and Swinbank 2011: 66).

The influence of farm organizations was also favoured by the fact that, in political terms, the farm vote was not ideologically fragmented, but (on the contrary) clearly biased towards the centre-right. The electoral strategy of centre-right parties, largely successful during these years, included as a key point the mobilization of this loyal vote (Sheingate 2001: 127–180). Furthermore, in the socio-economic sphere, the rapid decline in farm-population numbers favoured the internal cohesion of the group and implied an equally rapid increase in the number of taxpayers and consumers over which the cost of farm-support policies could be diluted.

Considering these factors, for policymakers (at both national and European levels) it was crucial to secure support, or at least some consent, from the farm organizations. This also conditioned the CAP's policy process. For farm organizations, the essential point was to maximize farm support in the short run and, if possible, to provide farmers with good prospects in terms of security and growth. Therefore, their position on the CAP would be similar to the one they had held previously in national agricultural debates. They would favour price supports, with their necessary correlate of intervention buying, and repel any attempt on the part of policymakers to exchange this tangible, short-run support for uncertain, longer-term measures. Farm organizations were particularly hostile towards any structural measures that would allegedly correct the underlying productivity problem at the cost of expelling thousands of uncompetitive farmers from the sector (Tracy 1989: 362; Ackrill 2000: 200–201). An implication is that policymakers never felt that, in order to secure the backing from farm organizations, a system of agricultural support focused on small, low-income farmers had to be implemented. That sort of system would have fitted the notion of an agricultural welfare state, but it never found its way to the agenda of policymakers or farm organizations. The introduction of environmental or territorial criteria for the modulation of public support to farmers would never reach the agenda either.

This balance of interests among the EEC, member states and farm organizations remained more or less stable for a quarter century. This was made possible not only because of the internal consistency of the CAP as an expression of these interests, but also because of its external consistency in the eyes of public opinion. Broadly speaking, citizens were supportive of the values that inspired the CAP and failed to perceive the remarkable gap that existed between those values and the policy instruments that allegedly represented them. By the late 1980s, that is, at a time when the postwar cycle of widespread prosperity had been closed already and not few of the social wounds provoked by the industrial crisis of the 1970s were still open, the Commission's Eurobarometer showed that most Europeans were in favour of granting support to the agricultural sector but not to other sectors that also were in trouble, such as steel and shipbuilding (Commission of the European Communities 1988: IV). A far from negligible proportion of European citizens lacked an opinion on the CAP, but among those who did have an opinion, support for the CAP was strong (Table 5.1).

Once the original version of the CAP became fully shaped, this policy became very dependent on inertia, as the little success achieved by the Commission in

TABLE 5.1 Results of the 1987 Eurobarometer on the CAP (%)

		Mostly agree	*Mostly disagree*	*No answer*
"On balance the CAP is worthwhile"		46	18	36
	Enough	*Too small*	*Too big*	*No answer*
The agricultural budget is…	26	27	22	25

Source: Commission of the European Communities (1988: V, VIII).

its attempts to introduce structural measures or quantitative restrictions shows. Mansholt probably thought that, after the delicate issue of starting a common agricultural policy had been solved, he would be able to reorient the CAP in the direction he had always thought to be best. However, farm organizations reacted in a heated way to his vision of a European agriculture in which productivity gains would be reaped at the cost of deliberately inducing a drastic fall in the number of farmers. Moreover, after the "empty chair" crisis triggered by France during the implementation stage of the CAP, EEC governance rapidly evolved de facto towards a system in which any important decision would have to be reached by consensus of all member states, or otherwise it would be vetoed by any state that was not satisfied with it. Were this not enough, some states mistrusted the co-financing system that applied for structural measures or, simply, they had trouble securing the fiscal resources that were necessary in order to implement them properly. Mansholt's ideas, which did not fit well within the constellation of defensive values in which the European agricultural policy had come to be framed (Knudsen 2009a: 282–287), were then reduced to an extremely modest set of structural measures that, as we saw in Chapter 2, was never even close to attaining the budgetary relevance Mansholt had proposed.

Quantitative restrictions, on their part, were implemented in different versions during the 1980s, but farm organizations were openly against them because they (rightly) understood that in the short run those restrictions implied a cut in agricultural support. Food processors were also against quantitative restrictions, because their growth strategy, conditioned by the decreasing dynamism of European demand, had become more and more dependent on subsidized exports to non-EEC markets (Koning 2017: Chapter 6). Faced with this opposition, the Commission implemented quantitative restrictions but, save for a few exceptions, did so through soft instruments that did not provoke major alterations in the CAP.

The remarkable stability of the balance of interests reached by member states, the EEC and farm organizations, reinforced by the public opinion's diffuse consent, allowed the CAP's original paradigm to prevail until the MacSharry reform of 1992. This was a paradigm that based its social legitimacy on the identification of a number of agrarian problems (among them, especially the farm-income problem), but it had been crucially driven by other, different factors. The high instrumental value that policymakers attached to reaching some agreement on the CAP, as well as the biased interpretation of the agrarian problems posed by member states and farm organizations, prevented the original CAP from being a better policy.

The destabilization of the traditional equilibrium

If the EU, the member states and the farm organizations had reached a stable equilibrium around the classic CAP, how then did important reforms take place at a later stage? In 1992 and 2003, in particular, commissioners MacSharry and Fischler led substantial, controversial reforms. Not only that: they also established a new era in which change, rather than continuity, would be the new "normal" in the evolution of the CAP. All actors involved in the policy process accept today that every new budgetary cycle will bring about reforms in large or small measure; that is, one reform every seven years (or even less if, as was the case in 2003, the mid-term review has major consequences). In other words, from the stability of the classic CAP we have moved to steady change. Why?

The basic cause is that the traditional balance of interests began to break down in the late 1980s and no other alternative, stable equilibrium has been reached ever since. The key to this breakdown, in its turn, was the widening of the "policy venue" in which CAP decisions were made. The Commission, led by "political entrepreneurs" like MacSharry and Fischler, was able to bring new interests to the policy process, forcing member states and farm organizations to play their game in a less propitious playing field. These new interests were basically three: the commercial and industrial interests of Europe's economy as a whole, the interests of taxpayers (mediated by the interests of those member states that were net contributors to the EU budget), and the interests of environmental and ruralist groups.

The interests of the European economy as a whole became decisive as soon as agriculture was incorporated into the international trade negotiations that were taking place within the General Agreement on Tariffs and Trade (GATT). One reason why the classic CAP had remained stable was because the negotiations for the removal of trade barriers between approximately 1945 and 1985 had focused on the markets for manufactured products, which left countries (or, in this case, the EEC/EU) free to pursue the agricultural policies they felt were more suitable to their interests. Initially, the country that led the restoration of a pro-globalization agenda after 1945, the United States, had held a negative view of the protectionist agricultural policy that the six founding states of the EEC were planning to implement. By the time the EEC actually implemented the CAP, however, this view had become more nuanced. The CAP would undoubtedly make the access of American farmers to the European market even more difficult than it already was, but it would also contribute to consolidating the EEC. This, in turn, would contribute to the progress of the pro-trade agenda within Europe and, at a later stage, in the world at large. Once the United States was guaranteed that its companies would be able to access the European market for corn and soy (key inputs for the ongoing expansion of the European livestock sector), they gave the green-light to the CAP. The

GATT basically accepted the American analysis of the situation when it decided that regional processes of economic integration (among which the EEC was by far the most relevant) should be seen as instruments of progress towards international liberalization, rather than as sources of trade diversion that could harm third countries. Similar to the EEC and the member states, then, both the United States and the GATT came to accept the CAP for instrumental, rather than intrinsic, reasons (Coppolaro 2009; McMichael 2013: 37; González et al. 2016: 73–75).

In 1986, however, the Uruguay Round of the GATT positioned agriculture in the pro-trade agenda. For around twenty years, this put European policymakers under unusual pressure. The WTO, the successor organization to the GATT, even created (with technical assistance from the OECD) a methodology to classify policies according to their degree of distortion in international markets. The bulk of the classic CAP, with its strong market-intervention measures, was undoubtedly included in the so-called amber box, that is, on top of the list of highly distortive policies that should be dismantled or reformed in the short run. The implication was clear to Brussels: not every CAP would be valid anymore.

The shift of the GATT/WTO agenda had different causes, among them the general reorientation of Western economic policy towards the market after the crisis of the 1970s and subsequent difficulties in returning to a path of rapid growth. During those years, the evolution of the OECD agenda towards global liberalization is symptomatic of this trend (Schmelzer 2016: 54, 68). But, in relation to specifically agricultural factors, the main issue was that the classic CAP was damaging the trade interests of the United States to such an extent that the latter was unwilling to tolerate it anymore. While EU protectionism prevented most American farmers from accessing the European market, the EU had become a net exporter of the main products coming from temperate-climate agri-food systems: not only meat and dairy, but also cereals and its derivatives. Until then the leading position of the United States had been undisputed. The expansion of European exports in (for instance) the belt of cereal-importing countries in northern Africa was based on capturing shares of the market that previously had been American. Other developed countries with potentially competitive exporters, such as Australia and Canada, joined forces with the United States in the international attack against the CAP. The United States conceded so much importance to agricultural trade negotiations that it credibly threatened to collapse the whole Uruguay Round if a satisfactory outcome were not reached (Josling 1997: 360–364; Ackrill 2000: 95–103; Koning 2017: Chapter 7).

This gave political entrepreneurs like MacSharry and Fischler a perfect occasion to reincorporate broader commercial and industrial interests into the agricultural-policy process. In the past these interests had favoured an instrumental agreement about the original CAP, as we have seen. Now, however, they favoured an instrumental agreement about reforming it. In most countries, including France (and even more so Germany), the farm losses that a CAP reform could entail were clearly smaller than the benefits that the politicians and companies related to the non-farm economy expected to reap from a new round of international liberalization of the markets for industrial products. New policymakers, such as the EU trade commissioner or the national ministers of economy or foreign affairs, exerted a remarkable influence on the CAP's policy process, eroding what until then had been the preserve of agricultural policymakers and of the interest groups they were closely related to (Ackrill 2000: 174–175; Sheingate 2001: 214–219). In a way, this shows the limits of "developmental pattern": there came a time when the ever-decreasing socio-economic importance of the farm sector began to be detrimental, instead of favourable, to the power and influence of the agri-policy network.

Commissioners like MacSharry and Fischler mobilized these more general interests to reform the CAP and soften the international pressure upon it. MacSharry's payments, designed under the pressure of saving the Uruguay Round, could qualify as a "blue box" measure, that is, a measure linked to output or input but also to some commitment to setting land aside. Some years later, Fischler's payments, designed in anticipation of the next round of WTO negotiations, had the aspiration of entering the "green box", composed of support measures decoupled from production and prices, where they would be protected from any pressure for further reform. The new payments of the MacSharry and Fischler reforms, moreover, could be portrayed before the farm organizations as a tangible compensation for the gradual phasing out of high guaranteed prices. In the later part of the process, the agri-policy network came to accept this paradigm change in the CAP. After all, securing a system of direct payments was probably better for them than taking the risk of resisting change and witnessing the application (without any compensations) of low prices and quantitative restrictions in the framework of an unreformed CAP (Ackrill 2000: 174–175; Cunha and Swinbank 2011: 100–101, 148; Lovec 2016: 112, 132, 143).

It is true that in the past ten years or so the external pressure on the CAP has diminished. Conditioned by political resistance and social contestation in both the global North and the global South, the agricultural negotiations of the WTO's Doha Round reached a deadlock in the early years of the new millennium (Pritchard 2009). More recent events, such as the rise to power of Donald Trump (the first US president who does not share the pro-globalization agenda of the Bretton Woods institutions), move us further away from the possibility that national agricultural policies become exposed again to powerful external pressures in the short run. But, precisely for that reason, this allows us to perceive that the two most profound reforms of the CAP (MacSharry in 1992 and Fischler in 2003) took place in the interlude during which said pressures were very intense.

Alongside external pressure, the destabilization of the classic CAP and the opening up of a new phase of steady reform were also related to the incorporation of taxpayers' interests into the policy process. This happened indirectly, through the interests of the member states that were net contributors to the EU budget. In the 1980s, both the Commission and the contributor states began to feel uncomfortable with what seemed to be an uncontrolled rise in CAP expenditure. This was partly the legacy of the 1970s, when price policy had been generous and there were no quantitative restrictions but, during the 1980s, neither a more austere price policy nor the introduction of soft quantitative restrictions had been able to stop total CAP expenditure from growing (Tracy 1989: Chapter 14). Furthermore, the EU's successive enlargements towards the Mediterranean and Central and Eastern Europe made the CAP's budgetary prospects even bleaker: the new member states would be net recipients and, especially in the cases of Spain and Poland, would bring a large number of farmers into the EU's regulatory system (Ackrill 2000: 77–92; Swinnen 2008).

On the other hand, these budgetary pressures on the CAP were unfolding at a time when the instrumental content of this policy, so preciously esteemed by a previous generation of politicians, was devaluating (Ludlow 2009). European integration had become a consolidated political project in which new policies were being implemented, so that a now not-so-irreplaceable CAP had to face more competition over the EU's limited budget resources than in the past. The most important of these new policies was the regional cohesion policy, which was oriented towards the promotion of socio-economic development in the most backward regions of the EU. Undoubtedly, this was a policy with more social visibility than the CAP. Why, the Commission began to wonder, allocate such a large share of the EU budget to the CAP?

It is likely that the discourse on the CAP's lack of budgetary viability - in the terms in which it has been posed recurrently in the European debate since the 1980s – has fallen prey to exaggeration. In retrospective, even the participants in the policy process admit that international pressures coming from the GATT and the WTO were more crucial at triggering reform than were internal concerns about the budget (Cunha and Swinbank 2011: 160–161). MacSharry even once declared that "the question of how much is spent is less important than how it is spen[t,] and we must have a policy that gives value for money" (cf. Cunha and Swinbank 2011: 88) – a statement really hard to imagine from a policymaker who had been truly facing a dramatic budgetary crisis. The CAP began to exert strong pressure on the EU budget not only because of its own problems, but also because the budget was actually tiny. It was not until 1988, for instance, that member states reached an agreement to create a funding instrument based on each country's GDP. It is not at all obvious that the classic paradigm of the CAP was doomed to generate an increase in expenditure. If it eventually did, it was because the Commission was, except for a few exceptions, unable to overcome the opposition of farm organizations and food industries (partly mediated through the opposition of key member states) to implementing hard quantitative restrictions. In other words, it is not at all obvious that budgetary pressures required reforms such as the ones led by MacSharry or Fischler. In fact, the MacSharry reform implied the transition towards a system of direct subsidies that, 30 years earlier, in the discussions about the original CAP, had been considered unviable for budgetary reasons (Tracy 1989: Chapter 12; Malassis 1997: 196; Milward 2000: 254–255; Knudsen 2009a: 146–148).

In any event, whether by means of hard restrictions (difficult to defend in the international arena) or by means of direct subsidies increasingly decoupled from production, the Commission and the member states that were net contributors needed a CAP with predictable budgetary implications. They also needed these implications to be autonomous from whatever decisions farmers could take in response to agricultural policy itself. This is the angle from which the budgetary pressures generated by the classic CAP can be seen as a motivating, rather than determinant, pro-reform factor (Ackrill 2000: 106; Cunha and Swinbank 2011: 86–92).

Finally, a third force contributing to destabilization of the traditional equilibrium reached regarding the classic CAP was the incorporation of new, non-farm interest groups into the policy process. There were basically two types: on the one hand, environmental organizations that, in the new social constellation taking shape after 1968/73, vindicated an agricultural policy that ceased promoting productivism and started promoting sustainable farming instead; on the other, "ruralist" groups that, following the creation of local action groups by LEADER in the 1990s, vindicated a reorientation of the CAP from agricultural subsidies towards rural development. Moreover, during the 1990s these new interest groups were joined by a renewal of the agrarian ideas of the European left, at a time when it was recovering much of its electoral clout. The new ideas of the European left included social democratic proposals to focus support on small farmers and green proposals to strengthen the link between agricultural subsidies and environmental sustainability (Koning 2017: Chapter 7).

The emergence of new interest groups and new political ideas allowed member states, and especially the Commission, to face their negotiations with farm organizations from a more autonomous position than in the past. This allowed for the introduction in the CAP of social, environmental and territorial criteria that otherwise would have been too openly at odds with farm organizations' demands for unfocused, unconditional farm support. In fact, the political entrepreneurs in search of reforms deliberately sought to mobilize the new interests in order to displace the debate towards a policy venue that was less favourable to farm organizations (Swinnen 2008). Fischler, for instance, contributed crucially to strengthening and uniting the very diffuse ruralist interest groups, which otherwise would have never been able to play a notable role in the policy process.

Farm organizations, then, found themselves in a weaker position than in the past (Ackrill 2000: 175–176). In the case of COPA, what had traditionally been an almost quotidian relationship with the Commission staff in order to perform co-management tasks became a more distant relationship – one that remained fluid, but was more spaced in time and rather limited to consultation (Cunha and Swinbank 2011: 66; Lovec 2016: 29, 98). With agricultural support threatened by budget cuts, and with national agricultural politicians ever more cornered within their own governments, farm organizations came to accept the discursive proposal the Commission offered them around the turn of the millennium: to stress the multifunctionality of the "European model of agriculture" – that is, the environmental and territorial contributions that farmers made in a society that was already very different from that of the postwar decades. At the beginning of the era of reforms, it had been common for organizations like (for instance) the French FNSEA to proclaim, "[we] do not want social supports, we want to make our income in the market" (cf. Lovec 2016: 101). Now, those attempts of holding on to the classic paradigm of the CAP were left behind. It was time to forge a temporal alliance with environmentalists and ruralists in a sort of pro-CAP front that, in order to keep the agricultural budget safe from the attacks led by non-farm and non-European interests, agreed to substitute unconditional support with focalized subsidies (Swinnen 2008).

None of this amounted to achieving a stable equilibrium to replace that of the classic CAP. Even once the external pressure on the CAP eased off, the budget debate within the EU has managed to maintain the pro-reform momentum. The "budget for reforms" transaction has been accepted as a permanent playing field for all participants in the definition of each seven-year budgetary cycle. The transition towards a system of direct subsidies need not imply a reduction in farm support (as MacSharry repeatedly stressed), but it did increase the latter's "budget exposure" (Sheingate 2001: 208–209). That is, it turned support more transparent and, therefore, more amenable to later attacks in the name of taxpayers' interests. The coalition between farm organizations and the new interest groups (environmentalists in particular) is not stable either, as was shown by its breakdown during the negotiations for the 2014–2020 CAP (Swinnen 2015). And yet, this succession of unstable equilibriums has been enough to correct the most evident dysfunctionalities of the classic CAP.

Why has reform not been more substantial?

The preceding discussion should not lead us to idealize the EU's ability to redesign the CAP. In fact, and as we saw in Chapter 4, the CAP's results in terms of coordinated capitalism remain poor even after the wave of reforms that started in 1992. In spite of the introduction of some correcting coefficients, a substantial social modulation of subsidies has not happened, and most CAP expenditure is still absorbed by a very small number of large landowners, and not by the neediest farmers. In spite of the introduction of environmental criteria for the granting of direct payments, CAP expenditure remains strongly oriented towards conventional farmers, and not towards organic farmers. And, in spite of the creation of a second pillar in order to promote rural development, the first pillar remains dominant, and it is farmers (rather than the rural community as a whole) who most benefit from the second pillar. Each of these outcomes results from social, environmental and territorial criteria having been introduced in a very gentle way. In consequence, the CAP has not become an agricultural welfare state, a green policy or a pillar of rural development.

Why have the reforms not been more substantial? The short answer is that, for different reasons, the Commission has been incapable of securing enough support from farm organizations and, more importantly, from member states. The Commission, whose members are only weakly conditioned by partisan or national interests, has taken the initiative in all three areas. It has even won a few battles in each of them: creating the second pillar in 1999, making the social modulation of subsidies compulsory for all member states in 2003, or creating a "green payment" as one of the two major payment regimes of the CAP's first pillar in 2014. However, in each of the three areas the Commission has been forced to accept substantial cuts and changes in its initial proposals – as a result of resistance, inertia and (not unfrequently) direct opposition on the part of the other participants in the policy process.

The most frontal opposition to change has been that of farm organizations. It is true that the agricultural interest groups have embraced the multifunctionality discourse, leaving behind their traditional reluctance to have farmers presented as countryside stewards instead of as food producers. In practice, however, farm organizations lobby for an outcome as similar as possible to their underlying ideal of widespread, unconditional support. From their point of view, any substantial focalization according to social, environmental or territorial criteria would imply a tightening of the conditions necessary for farmers to benefit from public support. For that reason, it would also favour that support, featuring a high degree of budget exposure, to be cut back at a later stage. The Commission's social modulation proposals have always been about penalizing large farmers rather than rewarding the smaller ones. The current green payment is designed more as a punishment to farmers who do not undertake sustainable practices than as a reward for those who do. And, if the second pillar focused exclusively on promoting economic diversification and the rural quality of life, this would only happen at the expense of funds that were previously going to farmers. Whatever the method chosen for the focalization of subsidies, any substantial focalization will generate a large group of farmers who would be directly harmed by reform. And that is precisely what the farm organizations, for reasons of internal cohesion that bring to mind those that led them to favour price supports over structural measures in the classic era of the CAP, try to avoid. COPA's strategy, a combination of rhetorical adhesion to the notion of the European model of agriculture and a patent lack of practical interest in the social modulation of subsidies or in rural development (Cunha and Swinbank 2011: 123), is illustrative in this regard.

Farm organizations have proven to be insightful when it comes to identifying the instrumental concessions that will contribute to the maintenance of agricultural support and telling them from the ones who will not. A good example is given by their position in relation to the "greening" of the CAP projected by Commissioner Cioloş for the period 2014–2020. During negotiations prior to 2014, farm organizations showed only some support for environmental criteria for as long as the funding of the CAP within the EU budget was under threat. As soon as the budgetary debate was resolved in not too unfavourable a sense, they broke what until then had been a pro-green CAP coalition with environmental organizations (Swinnen 2015).

Additionally, the capacity of resistance displayed by farm organizations is amplified by the increasing decentralisation of the decision-making process. The European Parliament has come to have co-decision powers over the CAP. Its reports and positions are not merely consultative anymore: they are an integral

part of the CAP's redesign process. But this, which we would in principle associate with a healthy trend towards democratization (the Parliament being the
only EU institution whose members are elected directly by the citizens), has
strengthened the lobbying influence of farm organizations (Cunha and Swinbank
2011: 96; Swinnen 2015; Lovec 2016: 30–33). The time required for the comple-
tion of any reform process has increased, which has given farm organizations more
room to forge alliances and responses to any unfavourable proposals posed by the
Commission. This contrasts with the radicalism of those reforms that, as was the
case with MacSharry in 1992 and Fischler in 2003, were completed in periods
that all participants in the process found surprisingly short, following a longer but
mostly secret period of painstaking preparation of the reform by a hard core of
Commission staff (Ackrill 2000: 179; Swinnen 2008: 137–138). The incorporation
of the parliament to the decision-making process has also made it easier for farm
organizations to access key actors from the political network. Most of these are
EU members of parliament who are involved in agricultural committees and have
a previous history of negotiation with farm organizations on a national scale. To
this we must add the "re-nationalization" of the CAP, which increases the decision
power of national and regional policymakers who are more easily accessible than
its EU-level counterparts.

Yet, these national and regional policymakers must be seen as political actors
with motivations that go beyond simply consenting to the demands made by farm
organizations. Farm organizations are not, after all, as powerful as they were in
the days of the classic CAP. Why, then, have states been less supportive than the
Commission to the idea of introducing social, environmental and territorial criteria
in the CAP? Why have they often watered down, or even blocked, many of the
Commission's proposals? Although resistance to change among farm organizations
is stronger, resistance to change among member states is probably more relevant.

A major cause of member states' resistance to change is that they have come to
perceive the CAP (and the EU more broadly) as a "gigantic redistribution machine"
(Patel 2009: 160). This generates "status quo bias" (Sheingate 2001: 219–222).
States have been enormously reluctant to any change in the political and economic balances that keep them together within the EU. In the particular case of
the CAP, if farm organizations are reluctant to focalize because this would create a
group of easily identifiable losers, national politicians can become even more reluctant if they perceive that those losers would be overrepresented in their country
and that, therefore, a lower amount of CAP funds would be allocated to their
country. Avoiding this scenario is rapidly perceived by national ministers as the key
to satisfying not only the farm organizations in their respective countries, but also
public opinion. Public opinion has eventually converged with national politicians
in their view of the CAP as a redistribution machine. Successfully negotiating CAP
reforms basically means to attract the largest possible amount of funds for one's own
country. This strongly conditions the range of positions that a national politician
will identify as leading them to a relatively safe path of career advancement. In consequence, reforms can only take place within the parameters fixed by pre-existing

TABLE 5.2 Share of CAP expenditure absorbed by the largest member states (%)

	France	Germany	Italy	Poland	Spain	United Kingdom
1989/91	20	15	17		9	7
1999/2001	22	15	13		15	10
2008	21	13	12	3	14	8
2017	18	11	10	8	13	7

Sources: Vega (2005: 106); European Commission (2009, 2018a).

intergovernmental balances, which have in fact remained remarkably stable over time (Table 5.2; see also Kay 2006: 90–103).

Why, for instance, has it been so hard for the Commission to persuade member states to apply modulations that would allow small farmers to benefit from the CAP more than proportionately? Among other reasons, because it had to face the frontal opposition of countries such as Germany and the United Kingdom, where the proportion of large farms was greater than the EU average and, therefore, a social modulation of subsidies would entail a reduction in their respective "national envelopes" (Cunha and Swinbank 2011: 120, 133). In other countries, like Spain, the exploitation of the redistribution machine has ramified on a regional scale. Because agrarian structures are very heterogeneous among Spanish regions, focalizing support on small farmers would have provoked substantial changes in the regional distribution of CAP funds. Some of the countries' most backward regions, such as Andalusia, would have lost out because their agrarian structure is dominated by large estates and *latifundia* (Compés 2006: 49). It is disputable that, as Knudsen (2009a: 296–297) proposes, these resistances to modulation reflect the persistence of the universalism ideals of the welfare state that triumphed in the 1960s. It rather seems that the social democratic ideal of reorienting the CAP in a pro-equality direction has tended to dilute time and again in the game of national and regional rivalries.

The status quo bias is further reinforced by the EU's governance system. The classic system, based on consensus decision-making as a means to avoid vetoes from individual countries, biased the pace and content of reform towards the interests of those states that, at any given moment in time, positioned themselves as the fiercest opponents of the Commission's reform proposal (Acrkill 2000: 180). With the shift to a system of qualified majority voting, this bias has moderated (Swinnen 2008), but the interests of the hypothetical losers from reform remain strongly over-represented in relation to interests of the hypothetical winners. If a state as prominent As France belongs to the group of hypothetical losers (which is often the case, given the country's persistent first place in the ranking of receivers of CAP funds), it is especially difficult for the Commission to get its proposals passed without substantial changes. The tense relationship between France and the Commission during the minor reform of 1999, which France basically succeeded at emptying

TABLE 5.3 Results of the 2017 Eurobarometer on the CAP's degree of success at meeting the following objectives (%)

	Agree	Disagree	Don't know
Ensuring a fair standard of living for farmers	56	30	14
Protecting the environment and tackling climate change	57	30	13
Creating growth and jobs in rural areas	52	33	15

Source: European Commission (2018b: 11).

out of its main content, and the major reform of 2003, during which France was able to secure significant concessions (for instance, the possibility of keeping a proportion of its subsidies indirectly coupled to production), gives a good illustration (Fischler 2011: vi).

As was already the case during the classic era of the CAP, the resulting policy outcome is in large measure endorsed by a public opinion that does not necessarily perceive the gap between discourse and reality. The reality of the reforms that started in 1992 has fallen short of the EU's discourse on social justice, environmental sustainability or territorial cohesion, but in any of these three areas citizens think that, broadly speaking, the CAP is fulfilling its role satisfactorily (Table 5.3). Of course, this does not put policymakers under much pressure when it comes to questioning the limits of the CAP's current paradigm and promoting policy changes that more vigorously support small farmers, organic farmers and rural entrepreneurs.

Conclusion

Opinion surveys past and present portray European citizens as reasonably satisfied with the EU's orientation towards supporting farmers, protecting the environment and promoting rural development. Policymakers past and present have also been reasonably inclined to do something about these matters. And, yet, why has the final outcome been so disappointing? Why has the CAP failed to illustrate the alleged virtues of coordinated capitalism? Basically, because from very early on its policy process – based on the interaction between the EU, member states and farm organizations – branched off the trajectory that was needed. This also had an impact on the direction taken by later rounds of reform, in which the sectoral and national interests created by each previous version of the CAP made manifest the legacy of the past. Path dependency has prevented the CAP from ever coming close to what supporters of coordinated capitalism would hope for.

However, this path-dependent story is essentially different to the account that we find in the first generation of rational-choice models, according to which powerful farm organizations capture policymakers and make them implement a clientelist policy that is prejudicial to the (more diffuse) interests of a mass of non-farm citizens. The explanation given in this chapter is different in two senses. First, it pays more attention to the supranational and intergovernmental context of the CAP's decision-making process. Understandably, the first generation of rational-choice models took the state as its reference framework but, precisely because of that, its contributions cannot be automatically transferred to the context of European integration. The original CAP was in large measure a Europeanization of the market-intervention policies that member states had for some time already been applying on their own, as well as of the values that officially informed said policies. Therefore, and beyond the lobbying influence of farm organizations, the balances of power between various member states and between member states and the Commission had a decisive impact on the final outcome. These balances have also been crucial for the making of a new CAP paradigm from 1992 onwards. In fact, during the last quarter century farm organizations have become clearly less influential than in the past and, yet, intergovernmental tensions and the characteristics of the EU's governance system have done much to dilute the content of reforms.

The story told in this chapter is different in a second sense, too: it opens up more space for the emergence of disruptive forces. Even if these forces are unable to eliminate path-dependent inertia completely, they do have the power to destabilize political equilibriums and, under certain circumstances, may even lead to paradigm change in agricultural policy. Contrary to the image of a clientelist policy that helplessly perpetuates itself over time (because it creates vested interests and little incentive for policymakers to attack them), historical institutionalism stresses that political entrepreneurs may try to mobilize non-farm interests in order to trigger policy reform. This is basically what happened with the CAP in 1992 and 2003, when commissioners MacSharry and Fischler mobilized the interests of nonmember countries (the United States in particular), the manufacturing sector, taxpayers and environmental organizations in order to destabilize CAP's traditional equilibrium.

The problem, from the viewpoint of this book's argument, is that the earthquake caused by these disruptive forces had very significant effects on the instruments of agricultural policy, but they did not trigger a substantial reorientation of those instruments towards social justice, environmental sustainability or rural development.

References

Ackrill, R. 2000. *The Common Agricultural Policy*. Sheffield: Sheffield Academic Press.

Anderson, K., Rausser, G., and Swinnen, J. 2013. "Political economy of public policies: Insights from distortions to agricultural and food markets". *Journal of Economic Literature* 51 (2): 423–477.

Brassley, P., Martiin, C., and Pan-Montojo, J. 2016. "Similar means to secure postwar food supplies across Western Europe". In *Agriculture in capitalist Europe, 1945–1960: From food shortages to food surpluses*, eds. C. Martiin, J. Pan-Montojo and P. Brassley, 271–274. Farnham: Ashgate.

Buckwell, A. 1997. "Some microeconomic analysis of CAP market regimes". In *The Common Agricultural Policy*, eds. C. Ritson and D. R. Harvey, 139–162. Wallingford: CAB International.

Commission of the European Communities. 1988. *Eurobarometer – Europeans and their agriculture*. Luxembourg: Directorate-General Information, Communication, Culture.

Compés, R. 2006. "Los principios básicos de la reforma 'intermedia'". In *La reforma de la Política Agraria Común: preguntas y respuestas en torno al futuro de la agricultura*, coord. J. M. García Álvarez-Coque, 35–60. Madrid: Eumedia and Ministerio de Agricultura, Pesca y Alimentación.

Coppolaro, L. 2009. "The Six, agriculture, and GATT. An international history of the CAP negotiations, 1958–1967". In *Fertile ground for Europe? The history of European integration and the Common Agricultural Policy since 1945*, ed. K. K. Patel, 201–219. Baden-Baden: Nomos.

Cunha, A. and Swinbank, A. 2011. *An inside view of the CAP reform process: Explaining the MacSharry, Agenda 2000, and Fischler reforms*. Oxford: Oxford University Press.

de Gorter, H. and Swinnen, J. 2002. "Political economy of agricultural policy". In *Handbook of agricultural economics, volume 2B: Agricultural and food policy*, eds. B. L. Gardner and G. C. Rausser, 1893–1943. Amsterdam: Elsevier.

de Grazia, V. 2005. *Irresistible empire: America's advance through twentieth-century Europe*. Cambridge: Belknap Press.

Eichengreen, B. 2007. *The European economy since 1945: Coordinated capitalism and beyond*. Princeton: Princeton University Press.

European Commission. 2009. *Annexes to the Commission working staff document accompanying the 2nd Financial Report from the Commission to the European Parliament and the Council on the European Agricultural Guarantee Fund – 2008 financial year*. Brussels: European Commission.

European Commission. 2018a. *Commission staff working document accompanying the document Report from the Commission to the European Parliament and the Council on the European Agricultural Guarantee Fund – 2017 financial year*. Brussels: European Commission.

European Commission. 2018b. *Special Eurobarometer 473: Europeans, agriculture and the CAP*. Luxembourg: Office for Official Publications of the European Communities.

Fernández, E. 2016. "Politics, coalitions, and support of farmers, 1920–1975". *European Review of Economic History* 20 (1): 102–122.

Fioretos, O., Falleti, T. G., and Sheingate, A. 2016. "Historical institutionalism in political science". In *Oxford handbook of historical institutionalism*, eds. O. Fioretos, T. G. Falleti and A. Sheingate, 3–30. New York: Oxford University Press.

Fischler, F. 2011. "Foreword: The CAP – a fundamental pillar constructing the 'European house'". In *An inside view of the CAP reform process: Explaining the MacSharry, Agenda 2000, and Fischler reforms*, A. Cunha and A. Swinbank, v–vii. Oxford: Oxford University Press.

González, Á. L., Pinilla, V., and Serrano, R. 2016. "International agricultural markets after the war, 1945–1960". In *Agriculture in capitalist Europe, 1945–1960: from food shortages to food surpluses*, eds. C. Martiin, J. Pan-Montojo and P. Brassley, 64–84. Farnham: Ashgate.

Hill, B. 2011. *Understanding the Common Agricultural Policy*. London: Routledge.

Josling, T. 1997. "The CAP and North America". In *The Common Agricultural Policy*, eds. C. Ritson and D. R. Harvey, 359–375. Wallingford: CAB International.

Kay, A. 2006. *The dynamics of public policy: Theory and evidence*. Cheltenham: Edward Elgar.

Knudsen, A.-C. L. 2009a. *Farmers on welfare: The making of Europe's Common Agricultural Policy*. Ithaca, NY: Cornell University Press.

Knudsen, A.-C. L. 2009b. "Ideas, welfare, and values. Framing the Common Agricultural Policy in the 1960s". In *Fertile ground for Europe? The history of European integration and the Common Agricultural Policy since 1945*, ed. K. K. Patel, 61–78. Baden-Baden: Nomos.

Koning, N. 2017. *Food security, agricultural policies and economic growth: Long-term dynamics in the past, present and future*. London: Routledge.

Lanero, D. 2018. "La historiografía sobre las políticas agrarias en Europa occidental y España (1945–1960): una aproximación". In *Del pasado al futuro como problema: la historia agraria contemporánea española en el siglo XXI*, eds. D. Soto and J. M. Lana, 257–284. Zaragoza: Prensas Universitarias de Zaragoza.

Lindert, P. H. 1991. "Historical patterns of agricultural policy". In *Agriculture and the state: Growth, employment, and poverty in developing countries*, ed. C. P. Timmer, 29–83. Ithaca, NY: Cornell University Press.

Lovec, M. 2016. *The European Union's Common Agricultural Policy reforms*. London: Palgrave Macmillan.

Ludlow, N. P. 2009. "The green heart of Europe? The rise and fall of the CAP as the Community's central policy, 1958–1985". In *Fertile ground for Europe? The history of European integration and the Common Agricultural Policy since 1945*, ed. K. K. Patel, 79–96. Baden-Baden: Nomos.

McMichael, P. 2013. *Food regimes and agrarian questions*. Winnipeg: Fernwood.

Malassis, L. 1997. *Les trois âges de l'alimentaire. Essai sur une histoire sociale de l'alimentation et de l'agriculture, II: L'âge agro-industriel*. Paris: Cujas.

Milward, A. S. 2000. *The European rescue of the nation-state*. London: Routledge.

Olson, M. 1990. "Agricultural exploitation and subsidization: there is an explanation". *Choices* 4: 8–11.

Patel, K. K. 2009. "Europeanization *à contre-cœur*. West Germany and agricultural integration, 1945–1975". In *Fertile ground for Europe? The history of European integration and the Common Agricultural Policy since 1945*, ed. K. K. Patel, 139–160. Baden-Baden: Nomos.

Pritchard, B. 2009. "The long hangover from the second food regime: A world-historical interpretation of the collapse of the WTO Doha Round". *Agriculture and Human Values* 26 (4): 297–307.

Schmelzer, M. 2016. *The hegemony of growth: The OECD and the making of the economic growth paradigm*. Cambridge: Cambridge University Press.

Sheingate, A. D. 2001. *The rise of the agricultural welfare state: Institutions and interest group power in the United States, France, and Japan*. Princeton: Princeton University Press.

Spoerer, M. 2015. "Agricultural protection and support in the European Economic Community, 1962–92: Rent-seeking or welfare policy?". *European Review of Economic History* 19: 195–214.

Swinnen, J. F. M. 2008. "The political economy of the Fischler reforms of the EU's Common Agricultural Policy: The perfect storm?". In *The perfect storm: The political economy of the Fischler reforms of the Common Agricultural Policy*, ed. J. F. M. Swinnen, 135–166. Brussels: Centre for European Policy Studies.

Swinnen, J. F. M. 2015. "An imperfect storm in the political economy of the Common Agricultural Policy". In *The political economy of the 2014–2020 Common Agricultural Policy: An imperfect storm*, ed. J. F. M. Swinnen, 443–484. Brussels: Centre for European Policy Studies.

Swinnen, J. 2018. *The political economy of agricultural and food policies*. New York: Palgrave Macmillan.

van Merriënboer, J. 2009. "Commissioner Sicco Mansholt and the creation of the CAP". In *Fertile ground for Europe? The history of European integration and the Common Agricultural Policy since 1945*, ed. K. K. Patel, 181–197. Baden-Baden: Nomos.

Vega, J. 2005. "¿Quiénes son los verdaderos beneficiarios de la PAC?". In *Política agraria común: balance y perspectivas*, coords. J. L. García Delgado and M. J. García Grande, 100–123. Barcelona: La Caixa.

Thiemeyer, G. 2009. "The failure of the Green Pool and the success of the CAP: Long-term structures in European agricultural integration in the 1950s and 1960s". In *Fertile ground for Europe? The history of European integration and the Common Agricultural Policy since 1945*, ed. K. K. Patel, 47–59. Baden-Baden: Nomos.

Tracy, M. 1989. *Government and agriculture in Western Europe, 1880–1988.* New York: New York University Press.

EPILOGUE

A story to be continued?

"A story to be continued" is the subtitle of the little book published by the European Commission (2012) in order to celebrate the CAP's 50th anniversary. But, does this story really have to continue? And, if so, in what terms? This epilogue provides a conclusion to the book by bridging past, present and future. We will begin with a historical synthesis of the CAP in which the conclusions from the previous chapters are integrated in a chronological narrative. Next, we will explore where this history of the CAP leaves us in terms of the debate on coordinated capitalism and the European economic and social model. Finally, this arrow of time is projected onto the future in order to contextualize some policy recommendations.

Looking back

During its classic era, between its creation in 1962 and the MacSharry reform of 1992, the CAP did not lead to the making of a reliable model of agrarian coordinated capitalism in the EEC. Seen from this perspective, it was a missed opportunity. Even though the market intervention system implemented by the EEC contributed to sustaining the income of countless family farmers, its main outcome was to transfer public resources to large landowners and large business groups. Moreover, the classic CAP was without a doubt negative for the environment, as it gave farmers incentives to adopt productivist, unsustainable strategies. The classic CAP did not do much to strengthen Europe's territorial cohesion either, particularly in the area of reversing trends towards rural depopulation.

The price to be paid in order to realize these dubiously valuable benefits was far from negligible. The classic CAP led to a public expenditure climb that put the tiny EEC budget under strong pressure, extracted resources from consumers by fixing artificially high agricultural prices, and damaged the trade interests of third countries. Even so, those impacts were not the main problem with the classic CAP. After all, taxpayers never had to pay too much for the CAP, the undercover tax on food consumption did not prevent the culmination of the nutritional transition and the making of mass consumer society in Europe, and food systems in the global South suffered from endogenous problems that were more damaging than the CAP. The main problem is that the chief policy of the nascent EEC did not contribute clearly to a better society, standing thus in sharp contrast to the welfare-state polices that were being implemented (or reinforced) at that time on a national scale in areas such as education, health and social protection.

The cause of these mediocre results was that, even though the CAP was allegedly oriented towards the correction of social problems such as low farm incomes, its policy process early and persistently detoured from the path that could meet that objective. The policymakers and interest groups involved in the process succeeded at finding a consensus zone in which national agricultural support policies could be "Europeanized". This provided the European integration project with a material, tangible base to move forward. But this consensus zone, basically a market intervention policy based on high prices and on instruments to absorb (rather than to prevent) agricultural overproduction, was ill-suited for the development of something like a supranational agricultural welfare state.

The classic CAP remained stable for a quarter century, but in the late 1980s it began to be destabilized by the incorporation of new interests to its policy process. These included the United States' agri-exporting interests, the pro-trade interests of European manufacturing, the interests of European taxpayers (and net contributor member states), and new social sensibilities in relation to issues such as environmental sustainability and rural development. All of them stood in contradiction to the classic CAP.

A new era of periodic reforms was started, then, in order to accommodate these new interests with the interests represented by the classic CAP. Even though they were less stable than the traditional political equilibrium of the 1960s, 1970s and much of the 1980s, new political equilibria were reached. There were profound reforms in 1992 and 2003, as well as other reforms in 1999, 2007 and 2014. At the time of completing this book, in the autumn of 2019, a new reform is currently being discussed within the framework of the EU's new economic programming for the period after 2020. That the CAP will be redesigned to some extent for each seven-year budget period is something that all participants in the policy process, including farmers and farm organizations, have eventually had to come to terms with. So far, the common thread of the reforms has been the substitution of the EU's traditional instrument of farm support, market intervention, with a new instrument: direct payments to farmers. During the last quarter century, there has also been a trend towards decoupling direct subsidies from production and coupling them to social, territorial and (above all) environmental objectives.

These reforms have been enough to put most of CAP's negative impacts under control. The CAP's budget cost has stabilized. After the large farm population of Central and Eastern European entered the EU, the per capita cost of the CAP has actually decreased substantially. Agricultural prices in Europe have come quite close to world market prices, so that undercover taxation on food consumption has almost disappeared. The interests of third countries are viewed more respectfully and the EU has abandoned hard practices of unfair competition such as export subsidies. Traces of the CAP as an out-of-control monster are harder and harder to find.

The problem is that, nevertheless, reforms have not been successful at making the CAP's balance in terms of coordinated capitalism substantially better. The direct payments system kept most public support in the hands of a small number of large landowners, making any reference to an agricultural welfare state as untenable as in the past. The environmental focalization of subsidies mitigated some of the worst excesses committed by European farmers, but it basically played the part of bringing new legitimacy to a support pattern that went on subsidizing more or less the same farmers for undertaking more or less the same practices. The turn towards rural development, ultimately, was also unsuccessful. Even though genuine initiatives to promote local economic diversification were started, the funds allocated to rural development were actually very few and ended up being for the most part diverted to farmers, which made them of little use when it came to fighting depopulation and promoting local development.

Therefore, the social, environmental and territorial criteria brought about by the reforms of the last quarter century have been more rhetorical than real. This is partly due to the Commission's inability to prevent farm organizations and member states from watering down its starting proposals. Farm organizations have pragmatically embraced the new discourse on the post-productive functions of farming but, as soon as this discourse is effectively mobilized in order to secure funding for the CAP within EU budget debates, their objective is to get farm support to become as unconditional and widespread as possible. Member states, for their part, have been interested in the CAP first and foremost as a redistribution machine, rather than as a common policy oriented towards social, environmental and territorial objectives. This, combined with a governance system in which the interests of those countries that would be potentially worse off after a reform are over-represented, has greatly constrained the consensus zone in which reforms could proceed.

The CAP and the European model

The historical analysis performed in this book openly questions the discourse that the Commission has been generating about the CAP during the last half century. This discourse, which in large measure is accepted by public opinion, invites us to see the CAP as an illustration of the virtues of European-style coordinated capitalism — a variety of capitalism in which the state actively intervenes in order to pursue social, environmental and territorial objectives. The CAP, however, has not even come close to that ideal. In spite of the Commission's longstanding insistence on positioning it within the social-justice dimension intrinsic to the European welfare state, the CAP has never been focused on the neediest farmers, and its support has always been disproportionately captured by patrimonial and corporate elites. The (historically more recent) rhetoric of an environmental and territorial turn in the CAP does not correspond to reality either, as this policy has done little to promote organic farming or the economic development of rural communities. In fact, it is not at all clear that Europe has a truly distinctive agricultural policy, as the Commission so often proclaims. When, compared to the country that is most frequently invoked as the inverted image of Europe's socio-economic identity, the United States, it certainly does not.

Our analysis has also distanced itself from the liberal (in the sense of pro-free market) discourse on the CAP. According to this discourse, the CAP has always been a big mistake, explainable only because farm organizations have succeeded at having policymakers apply agricultural policies that are detrimental to the interests of most citizens. Liberal capitalism is superior to coordinated capitalism because it ensures a higher level of efficiency and, therefore, a higher level of welfare for society taken as a whole. Market intervention, particularly under the classic CAP, was a bureaucratic monster that had to be paid for by European consumers, European taxpayers and farmers in the rest of the world. And, if anything good can be said about the reforms starting in 1992, it is that these have been liberal reforms that have mitigated these diverse costs. However, and contrary to this train of thought, this book has argued that the costs of the CAP have never really been so excessive. The nutrition of Europeans was not substantially affected by the higher-than-equilibrium prices caused by the CAP's protectionism. The CAP has always represented a very small share of the public expenditure made in Europe and the EU has been able to contain its budget cost in spite of the incorporation of a very substantial number of farmers coming from the south and east of the continent. And it is doubtful that the CAP has had much to do with the problems of the poor farmers in the global South, for whom the anti-agrarian and anti-equality biases in their own national policies have been historically much more damaging. In this last respect, our analysis has also moved away from the proposals of Marxist sociologists and other critics of neoliberal globalization.

The main problem with the CAP was not, and is not, the negative impact it has, but the little positive impact it brings. The political-economy approach used throughout this book is receptive to the generic arguments in favour of coordinated capitalism, but our historical analysis concludes that said arguments do not really apply to the case of the CAP.

Where does this case study leave us in terms of the broader debates on the EU and the European economic and social model? To those of us who believe in the values that underpin the European model and the very process of European integration, it leaves us in an uncomfortable position. The debate tends to focus on whether or not the institutional arrangements of coordinated capitalism, the social value of which is commonly admitted, have a chance of surviving in an era marked by global liberalization and international competition. We pointed out at the beginning that some of the premises of this debate are questionable: for instance, the presentation of Europe's coordinated capitalism as an anomaly and the assumption of a link between competitiveness and innovation (on the one hand) and deregulation (on the other). But, moving one step further, the social value of European-style coordination cannot be taken for granted, either. What we find in this study case is an institutional arrangement that, in spite of being informed by political values widely shared by European citizens, is designed in a way that makes it enormously difficult for these values to leave their imprint in reality.

In other words, if the European model is this, then we would be better off without it. If European-style coordination always suffers from a gap as wide as this between rhetorical justifications and the real-world consequences of policies, then we are in need of a different kind of coordination for our capitalism. Of course, we should not presume that the CAP, with its peculiarities, is necessarily a representative case. But there are also other areas in the European model, such as labour-market regulation, taxation and social protection, for which similar doubts can be reasonably posed. Are the political values that inspire coordination well represented by the actually existing policies? Or, on the contrary, do these values form an ideological screen that citizens use as a substitute for a real analysis of policy options and results?

This leads us to the parallel debate on the degree to which the EU improves our lives. The EU project is a creature of the wide, centre-right and centre-left political spectrum that dominated the national politics of member states after the Second World War and in large measure continues to do so. This wide spectrum has tended to defend itself from the Eurosceptics' attacks by presenting them as crude populisms propagated by right-wing nationalism and the radical left. However, if we take the CAP as a reference point, what strikes as truly populist is the Commission's discourse past and present: fervent exposition of a series of political values, followed by a defence of policy solutions that are far too simple – or perhaps plain and simply wrong. Once the inspiring flags of social justice, environmental sustainability and territorial cohesion have been waved, and once they have been put in opposition to the allegedly neoliberal American alternative, public opinion becomes persuaded that these flags are well defended by means of a policy like the CAP. But, can we really close the farm income gap with farm subsidies and, even more dubiously, farm subsidies that go mostly to large landowners? Can we really fight climate change by introducing a few green, cosmetic retouches in that subsidy programme? Is giving money to farmers a way of fighting rural depopulation? And after all this […] it is the Eurosceptics who are supposed to be populists!

For different reasons, the wide spectrum of centre-right and centre-left political actors who have promoted and managed the European project have not succeeded at getting the CAP – for a long time the EU's main policy and still today its second most important policy in terms of expenditure – to keep up with the promise of the "European model". The centre-right has carried with it a burdensome tradition of close links with farm organizations that has deformed the policy process to the detriment of social, environmental and territorial objectives. The centre-left, in its turn, has not done much to reorient the process towards those objectives because, beyond rhetoric, it has found itself trapped by the so-called "national interests" and the logic of the CAP as a redistribution machine. How much can things change with the rise to power of a liberal centre that differentiates itself from the great conservative and social-democratic traditions? If we are to tell by the way in which, in the current round of CAP negotiations, Emmanuel Macron's France is reproducing positions and arguments that are reminiscent of those made by the French socialist government under MacSharry or the French conservative government under Fischler – not much.

When it comes to the CAP, some time has passed since we reached the point that historian Tony Judt (2011: 140) feared for the European project as a whole: the point when, after so much "[chanting] 'Europe' like a mantra, [...] we shall wake up one day to find that far from solving the problems of our continent the myth of 'Europe' has become an impediment to our recognizing them". Supporters of the EU make a strategic mistake when they insist that the CAP is a beautiful story to be continued. The CAP is actually a rather sad story. If all the stories that we can contrapose to Eurosceptic arguments are of this kind, no wonder Eurosceptics are ever more in number. What we need is that this sad story be discontinued.

Looking forward

Reflecting on second bests has become a politically pragmatic, academically popular activity. As we saw in Chapter 1, the transition to an era of steady reform has moved many researchers to focus on proposing changes that are feasible within the area made available by the policy process, regardless of their opinion about said area and said process. In other words, much research internalizes and naturalizes the political back room of the CAP and focuses on the practical task of discussing reform options that are simultaneously positive and plausible.

Nothing would be simpler than ending this book with one further exercise in CAP "deconstruction" (Compés 2010: 133–136). The arguments made in previous chapters open the way for suggestions in a number of directions. It would be good for the European Commission to lower the threshold for the social modulation of subsidies, so that subsidies benefit small farmers the most and the CAP gets closer to becoming an agricultural welfare state. The Commission should also more strictly define the environmental criteria involved in the perception of subsidies. Finally, the Commission should use the funds saved by these reforms (which would imply a penalty on the largest farmers and on those farmers who contribute to environmental protection the least) to strengthen the second pillar, which anyway should be reoriented towards economic diversification and the promotion of the rural quality of life. And, if the Commission is unable to pass just soft versions of these ideas, then member states should use their increasing room for manoeuvre to enforce harder versions.

As a matter of fact, the future of the CAP seems to go in that direction, especially when it comes to the environment. It is true that the social modulation of subsidies, after having been a hot issue during the 1990s, has lost momentum in the reformist agenda (Swinnen 2008). Rural development is not in its best moment either. The ruralist groups became important in the 1990s, as the LEADER initiative was spreading across the EU, but their influence soon reached a ceiling. Today they cannot aspire to much more than defending rural development from the collateral damage that budget cuts in the CAP may cause (Atance 2006).

But the environment is different. Environmental organizations have expanded and consolidated their power of influence because their cause is unambiguously backed by European public opinion. In fact, the Commission is tending more and more to position the CAP as a policy of natural-resource management and to fight against climate change. No doubt this is a deceiving positioning, but it illustrates well the extent to which, among the diverse discursive turns taken by CAP supporters, the environmental turn is the one that has become dominant. In the future, beginning with the currently ongoing reform for the period 2021–2027, it is almost certain that the trend towards coupling agricultural subsidies to environmental objectives will go on. The objectives will be defined more precisely and there will be a more complete list of indicators to monitor the environmental progress of the CAP.

The CAP will thus be a bit better and, consequently, its loss of budget share will be gradual only. In a way, a decreasing budget share will also act as an adjustment mechanism: some of the CAP's problems will be corrected and those that persist will become less relevant after every new assault on the agricultural budget by more-general interests. So, we are not precisely heading towards tragedy.

Yet, the promise of the "European model" deserves something better than merely avoiding the worst. The CAP, as we know it, should probably disappear and dissolve its components in more promising policy venues. Different instruments, as well as different political actors, are needed in order to make the promise of coordinated capitalism real.

This is particularly clear in the areas of environmental protection and territorial development. Rather than relying on the green retouches that agrarian policymakers may implement in a subsidy system the original design of which had nothing to do with the environment (Jones 2002), it seems more reasonable to insert agri-environmental measures within an integral approach to the sustainability of Europe's economy. It also seems more reasonable that, as has actually begun to be speculated about in the last few years, rural development measures become a part of the regional cohesion policy. That would be a more favourable policy venue for reorienting them towards the promotion of the non-farm sector of the rural economy and, more broadly, towards instruments that are more effective in the fight against rural depopulation and for an enhanced rural quality of life.

The role that the CAP has been playing from the start as an income policy for small farmers remains (by far) the most appropriate domain for agricultural policymakers to make their contribution to a better society. And yet, even in this domain it is likely that what we need is less a Common Agricultural Policy than a fully fledged Common Food Policy (de Schutter 2017). The economic support to small farmers should be part of a broader model of coordinated food capitalism. The starting point here should not be the problems of producers (these being farmers or processing companies), but the interest of consumers, not just in purely economic terms but also (and more importantly) in terms of food quality and nutritional health. Consumer interest should be met by a food chain capable of combining innovation and social cohesion. It is within this agenda that granting public support to small farmers makes sense. It is also within this agenda that debating effective policy instruments of farm support will be most productive. It is not obvious that direct subsidies support family farmers more effectively than an alternative based on a joint public–private coordination of the food chain. In any event, and similar to the cases of the environment and rural development, improving the social balance of the CAP also seems to require the incorporation of agricultural instruments and political actors within a policy venue that is wider than the current one.

We do not need the history of the CAP to continue. What we need is that the "European model" exists, works and gives us reason to remain together.

References

Atance, I. 2006. "El desarrollo rural". In *La reforma de la Política Agraria Común: preguntas y respuestas en torno al futuro de la agricultura*, coord. J. M. García Álvarez-Coque (coord.), 131–153. Madrid: Eumedia and Ministerio de Agricultura, Pesca y Alimentación.

Compés, R. 2010. "De la deconstrucción a la refundación: elementos para un cambio de modelo de reforma de la PAC 2013". In *"Chequeo médico" de la PAC y perspectivas de la Política Agraria Común tras 2013*, coords. J. M. García Álvarez-Coque and J. A. Gómez Limón (coords.), 129–153. Madrid: Eumedia and Ministerio de Medio Ambiente y Medio Rural y Marino.

de Schutter, O. 2017. "The political economy of food systems reform". *European Review of Agricultural Economics* 44 (4): 705–731.

European Commission. 2012. *The Common Agricultural Policy: A story to be continued.* Luxembourg: Office for Official Publications of the European Communities.

Jones, E. 2002. *The record of global economic development*. Cheltenham: Edward Elgar.

Judt, T. 2011. *A grand illusion? An essay on Europe*. New York: New York University Press.

Swinnen, J. F. M. 2008. "The political economy of the Fischler reforms of the EU's Common Agricultural Policy: The perfect storm?". In *The perfect storm: The political economy of the Fischler reforms of the Common Agricultural Policy*, ed. J. F. M. Swinnen, 135–166. Brussels: Centre for European Policy Studies.

INDEX

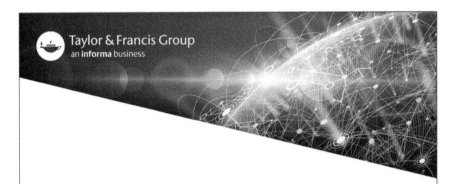

For Product Safety Concerns and Information please contact our EU
representative GPSR@taylorandfrancis.com
Taylor & Francis Verlag GmbH, Kaufingerstraße 24, 80331 München, Germany

www.ingramcontent.com/pod-product-compliance
Ingram Content Group UK Ltd.
Pitfield, Milton Keynes, MK11 3LW, UK
UKHW021848240425
457818UK00020B/765